Fight Back Against Unfair Debt Collection Practices

A partnership between American Library Association
and FINRA Investor Education Foundation

FINRA is proud to support the American Library Association

Fight Back Against Unfair Debt Collection Practices

Know Your Rights and Protect Yourself from Threats, Lies, and Intimidation

Fred Williams

Vice President, Publisher: Tim Moore
Associate Publisher and Director of Marketing: Amy Neidlinger
Executive Editor: Jeanne Glasser
Editorial Assistants: Myesha Graham and Pamela Boland
Development Editor: Russ Hall
Operations Manager: Gina Kanouse
Senior Marketing Manager: Julie Phifer
Publicity Manager: Laura Czaja
Assistant Marketing Manager: Megan Colvin
Cover Designer: Chuti Prasertsith
Managing Editor: Kristy Hart
Project Editor: Betsy Harris
Copy Editor: Karen Annett
Proofreader: Kathy Ruiz
Indexer: Angela Martin
Compositor: Nonie Ratcliff
Manufacturing Buyer: Dan Uhrig

© 2011 by Fred Williams
Published by Pearson Education, Inc.
Publishing as FT Press
Upper Saddle River, New Jersey 07458

FT Press offers excellent discounts on this book when ordered in quantity for bulk purchases
or special sales. For more information, please contact U.S. Corporate and Government Sales,
1-800-382-3419, corpsales@pearsontechgroup.com. For sales outside the U.S., please contact
International Sales at international@pearson.com.

Company and product names mentioned herein are the trademarks or registered trademarks
of their respective owners.

Printed in the United States of America

First Printing August 2010

ISBN-10: 0-13-705830-6
ISBN-13: 978-0-13-705830-3

Pearson Education LTD.
Pearson Education Australia PTY, Limited.
Pearson Education Singapore, Pte. Ltd.
Pearson Education North Asia, Ltd.
Pearson Education Canada, Ltd.
Pearson Educación de Mexico, S.A. de C.V.
Pearson Education—Japan
Pearson Education Malaysia, Pte. Ltd.

Library of Congress Cataloging-in-Publication Data

Williams, Fred O., 1961–
  Fight back against unfair debt collection practices : know your rights and protect yourself
from threats, lies, and intimidation / Fred Williams. — 1st ed.
    p. cm.
  ISBN 978-0-13-705830-3 (pbk. : alk. paper) 1. Collecting of accounts. I. Title.
  HG3752.5.W55 2010
  332.024'02—dc22
                            2010009638

Contents

Acknowledgments

The author wishes to thank the people of the Kiplinger Program in Public Affairs Journalism at The Ohio State University for their guidance and for supporting the research behind this book. The editors of *The Buffalo News* also provided support by granting time away from my role at the newspaper. In the course of the research, many individuals generously shared their time and expertise, in particular Robert J. Hobbs of the National Consumer Law Center.

Bob Frick at *Kiplinger's Personal Finance* magazine provided insights about publishing and connected me with my tireless agent, Grace Freedson. My colleagues Richard Haynes and Michelle Kearns read preliminary drafts and offered valuable advice, more of which I probably should have taken. Finally I wish to acknowledge my coworkers in debt collection, although I cannot name them without breaching their privacy. The time we spent working together shaped this book more than anything else.

About the Author

A business journalist for most of the past 24 years, **Fred Williams** has written about debt collection for *Kiplinger's Personal Finance* and for *The Buffalo (N.Y.) News*, where he started covering the industry in 1999. He undertook a six-month research project on the industry in 2006, supported by the Kiplinger Program in Public Affairs Journalism at The Ohio State University.

In 2008, he worked as a debt collector for 11 weeks at a collection agency near Buffalo.

Fred graduated from Binghamton University in 1986 with a bachelor's degree in economics. He currently lives in Charlottesville, Virginia, and is careful to pay his entire credit card balance each month.

Introduction

What got to me later was the answering machine greeting. It invited me to leave a message for Jim, Harley, or Bob—all men's names. I was looking for a woman named Samantha who owed $3,000 on a major credit card. The phone number I had dialed was the one on the account. As a debt collector, my first task was to call this number and demand payment. So, when the answering machine beeped, I took a breath and started to recite from a script thumbtacked to my cubicle. Halfway into my spiel about some "important business matter" that required Samantha's attention, Jim picked up.

Trying to get money from strangers is not my usual area of expertise. I had left my job as a newspaper reporter and gone to work at a collection agency to clear up a mystery. After reporting on the collection industry for years, I had heard countless stories about outrageous collection tactics. Debtors—or even people who did not owe money—recounted vicious threats and the lies that collectors used to squeeze them for cash. Their house would be seized, their family would be put on the street, or their children would watch as they were hauled off to jail. Around the nation, complaints like these are flooding into regulatory offices by the tens of thousands. Consumer advocates say the industry, lacking any real restraints, is descending into increasingly harsh—and more profitable—practices. Yet the collection industry claims there are only a few bad apples who don't represent the mainstream. Much of the griping comes from people who just don't like to pay their debts, the industry says.

Unsatisfied with that story, I decided that I had to work inside a mainstream collection agency to see what it was really like. That is how I found myself confronting Samantha about her $3,000 credit card bill—or rather, confronting her family. But why wasn't her name on the home answering machine?

"She died, finally," Jim said. "Last fall. We were estranged—she hasn't lived here in years. All that money you're looking for, she blew it. She put it up her nose."

His southern-accented voice was cordial, especially considering the number of stern-voiced collection calls he must have received by now. I could hear some grade-school-age kids playing in the background. Samantha's credit report was a black hole. She had signed up for any credit card that would have her, and charged each card up to the maximum. She also bounced checks, ignored her cell phone bill, and never paid a dime toward any of it. I asked Jim for the number on the death certificate, as I had been trained to do, and waited while he rooted around to find the document.

Unfortunately, my training also said that I must put the screws to Jim. His wife might have run up the bills. Or, being absent, she might simply be a convenient scapegoat. The credit card issuer didn't know, and it didn't have to. Jim was married to Samantha while the debt was being rung up. That, according to my training, put him on the hook for the $3,000, even though the law in his state might say otherwise. His wife's death made him my target.

After he read me the death certificate information, I asked him for the name of the executor, stalling for time. "Executor—you mean who buried her?" he said with a trace of scorn. "There wasn't no estate, if that's what you're getting at. All she left me was two boys to raise."

Two boys—they must be Harley and Bob. Now the answering machine greeting made sense. Samantha was out of the picture. Jim, Harley, and Bob, the little family she left behind, were getting along without her. For a moment, I didn't know what to say, a dangerous failure in my job. Jim could hang up at any moment. The children playing in the background now seemed to be arguing, their voices growing loud and strident.

I saw this job as a test. The question is: Can an honest collector abide by the law and still succeed? Industry representatives say that harsh tactics actually backfire. Telephone bullies need not apply. Instead, hard work and empathy are the keys to a collector's success. However, the collectors I know tell a different story. They say that the rules against using threats and lies are often ignored in the pursuit of the primary goal—bringing in money. To keep their jobs, they must meet targets measured in dollars each month.

As it turned out, the job tested more than the ability of a legally compliant collector to remain employed. On a day-to-day level, the job also tested my standards for reasonable and humane conduct. Living by the golden rule is not entirely congruent with the task of browbeating strangers who have fallen on hard times—especially ones whose lives have become a tragedy.

Jim stayed on the line, giving me my chance to demand the $3,000 from him. I couldn't do it. Instead, I mumbled something about the need to update our records. I got the name and number of Samantha's mother, the executor of her estate, and let Jim off the phone—and off the hook. I typed the code for "deceased" on the account. Then I slid off my headset, grabbed my coat, and stood up from my cubicle— really just a booth the size of a library carrel, with a phone and a computer terminal. I walked past row upon row of other stalls, past the whiteboard listing the dollar amounts that collectors had brought in that day, down the stairs, and outside into the gray, winter day.

A group of my coworkers stood there at the edge of the parking lot, chatting and smoking. It was break time; by chance, I had walked out of the building on the heels of everyone else. That was a lucky thing, or I would have walked off the job only a few days after starting it. Leaving work without permission is punishable by dismissal, especially for a trainee on probation.

"How's it going today?" my coworker Pamela asked, squinting at me. She might have seen the turmoil I felt. Pam is one of the more sensitive members of my trainee group; I have already figured her as one of those people who wouldn't meet the goals and would be ushered from the building at the end of our two-month probationary period, if not sooner. I told her about my call to Jim, Harley, and Bob's house and how I failed to even demand payment, my primary duty.

Her eyes widened and she blew out a puff of smoke derisively. "You hafta call them back," she said. "Not up to you to be saying who should pay, who doesn't." Getting a debtor on the phone only happens to us a few times a day, maybe once in every 25 phone calls. Having someone like Jim on the line and failing to demand payment is a tremendous waste: a waste of several hours of work, of the single daily call we're allowed to make to a debtor's home, of an opportunity that other collectors would be eager to make better use of.

I explained how Samantha had let her family down, and how I just couldn't bring myself to add to their problems. What they have to remember her by are the debts that trace her downfall and collection calls from people like me.

"So it makes you feel good to let these people believe they're better off than they are?" she demanded.

Well, yes—until she put it that way. Pam flicked her cigarette down and stubbed it with the toe of her boot. "Someone's going to get it out of them; only it won't be you," she concluded in a weary tone. "If you don't call them, I will."

By the end of the 15-minute break period, I made a deal with myself that allowed me to go back inside the building. I would give people like Jim a pass and pursue others extra hard, the deadbeats who run up charges and skip out, who leave town, and, indirectly, stick honest consumers with the bill. That's who I'll collect from, I told myself. The trouble is, these people are much harder to reach than sitting ducks like Jim.

Working as a reporter, I had seen how the availability of easy credit had transformed many people's lives into a modern form of debt bondage. People who ran up credit card bills became chained to an endless series of monthly payments, consisting mostly of interest. Debt collectors are the overseers in this system, the guards who keep the debtors in line. However, there are strong indications that the collection industry, or a substantial part of it, is no longer confined to this role as overseer.

Debt collectors caused more than 300,000 complaints to the Federal Trade Commission in the past five years, more than any other industry that the agency regulates.[1] The rate of complaints is exploding, having more than tripled since 2003. The number-one complaint is that collectors are demanding money that people do not even owe, even grabbing it directly from their bank accounts. As the industry casts its net wider and wider—making an estimated one billion contacts with consumers per year—a growing number of people say they are being shaken down by telephone bullies.

Consumer advocates say that threats and lies are rampant because toothless debtor protection laws make the tactics profitable.[2] The $1,000 federal civil penalty for collection abuses was set back in 1977, when Jimmy Carter was president. Since then, inflation has eroded the penalty while consumer credit has flourished. Seeing a golden opportunity, collection scams have launched brazen shakedown operations, fed by a wide-open market where they can buy old "debts" cheaply on an unregulated market. Their success puts pressure on mainstream agencies to match their strong-arm tactics or else lose business.

The collection industry denies that a wave of prohibited tactics is behind the surge in complaints. A minority of agencies are to blame for the outcry, the industry's lobbyists argue. They also point to rising debt levels and to consumers' simple irritation at being dunned as causes of the complaints. And there's plenty of irritation to go around these days, as the consumer debt bubble pops. Mortgage foreclosures and loan default rates have climbed to record levels. One in 45 homes received a foreclosure notice in 2009, according to Realty Trac's year-end report—quadruple the precrisis rate recorded in 2006. Meanwhile, the American Bankers Association's measure of consumer loan delinquencies set a record at the middle of 2009, "the cumulative effect of the longest recession since the Great Depression," Chief Economist James Chessen said. The U.S. consumer's love affair with easy credit is finally over, and the breakup is a bitter one. It will take years to pay off the overhang, which includes about $900 billion in credit card debt.[3]

Where does the truth lie? Are the complaints valid, or are they the groans of an overspent consumer class? The mounds of complaints lodged against collectors in courts and regulatory offices are surprisingly inconclusive. Faced with legal complaints brought under consumer protection law, collection agencies usually decide to settle, leaving the question of their guilt or innocence unanswered. The maximum $1,000 fine under the Fair Debt Collection Practices Act, the main consumer protection law governing debt collection, becomes a cost of doing business. Big cases brought by state and federal watchdog agencies yield higher penalties, but the same inconclusive result. NCO Group (formerly the National Collection Office, Inc.), the nation's largest collector, paid a $300,000 fine to the Pennsylvania attorney general in 2006 while denying any legal responsibility for the more than 800 complaints against it. Two years earlier, it had paid the Federal Trade Commission a fine of $1.5 million for passing false information about debtors to the credit reporting bureaus, while again denying guilt. In Illinois, a collection operation called Capital Acquisitions & Management (CAMCO) and its affiliates were able to settle FTC charges in 2004 by paying a fine and being shut down, after "threatening and harassing thousands of consumers," in the words of the FTC.[4]

For these complaints to be largely valid, as they seem to be, means there must be legions of people willing to do this sort of collection work. Who were they, I wondered, and what compelled them to make life miserable for others, day after day? To find out, I had to enter the industry and work alongside them, even become one of them. Both the debtors and the debt collectors described in the following pages are referred to by pseudonyms, to protect their privacy. For the same reason, the name of the collection agency I worked for is omitted and some of its identifying characteristics have been changed.

The following chapters describe what really goes on inside a mainstream collection agency. The tricks and tactics shown here illuminate Part 2, "Coping with Collections," which describes your rights under consumer protection law and how to protect yourself from unfair collection practices. Part 2 also details how to negotiate a debt settlement.

Working alongside debt collectors and learning their craft answered my questions about the industry's role in the modern system of debt bondage. However, if I had known the job would be this difficult—that I would have to make calls like the one to Jim, Harley, and Bob's house—I never would have started. This was not the only time I was ready to simply walk out of the building. But I had anticipated none of this before the first day on the job, when my training as a collector began.

Action Item: Identify the Collector

Your first step when a collector calls is to identify the agency you are dealing with. If a creditor has sent your bill to an outside collection agency, known as a third-party collector, you automatically have greater legal protection from tricks, threats, and harassment. This is because the Fair Debt Collection Practices Act covers third-party collectors, whereas it does not cover your primary creditor. Within five days of first contacting you, the collection agency is required to provide you with a *validation notice* stating the amount of the supposed debt, the original creditor, and the process for disputing the debt. For more information on identifying and backgrounding collection agencies, see Chapter 21, "Checking Out a Collector."

Part 1

Debt Collection Secrets

1

Lessons in Deception

It is 7:45 a.m. on a frigid January morning. I circle well to the rear of the parking lot behind the blocky office building. Spots near the front door are reserved for higher-ups, I was told during my interview for this job. So I park in the back, alongside domestic compacts like mine. Hardly any of them are adorned with bumper stickers or vanity plates. Maybe debt collectors don't like to call attention to themselves. The parking spots nearer to the entrance are crowded with SUVs.

Inside, 20 of us new hires stamp the snow off our boots, trudge up the stairs, and file into the training room. The classroom is partitioned off to one side of the collection "floor," a vast expanse that runs the length of the building's second story. On my way in, I watch an experienced collector wearing a wireless headset pace up and down an aisle, gesturing as he negotiates with a recalcitrant debtor.

The "floor" is where we all hope to arrive after our training. But many of us—most of us—will not make it. After a week of classroom instruction, we will go to cubicles set apart from the floor for a period of on-the-job training. There we will each have eight weeks to bring in $2,500 in "fee," or revenue for the agency. The fee on each amount collected is determined by the commission rate on the account. We can be fired for showing up late more than once, or for other minor infractions—and if we miss the $2,500 goal, we're history.

Most of my fellow trainees are men in their 20s and 30s, some in low-riding jeans and hoodies, a few in jackets and ties like me. I have the few items that the interviewer told me to bring: pen, highlighter, and picture ID. The ID is necessary to complete personnel forms. At least one of my colleagues has to fill out an extra form for people with a felony conviction on their record. As explained during the job interview, a criminal record doesn't preclude us from getting a job at this agency, as long as we disclose it.

Call centers are like factories used to be in this Rust Belt area—places where practically anyone can show up and get a job. But these jobs are easier to get than they are to keep. Of the four female trainees present at the start, one fails to return after the midmorning break, marking the first of what will be many abrupt exits from our group.

The training room walls have recently been painted yellow from shoulder level up, and people keep poking their heads in to comment on the fresh, chemical odor. "Good learning color," says one manager, my future boss, as she looks around at us, taking our measure. I sit at a computer terminal of age-yellowed plastic on which someone has written "upgrade me" with a thick black marker. The yellow walls are decorated with motivational posters. The nearest one shows a single crooked tree, clinging to a rock that sticks up out of the sea. The legend under the photo says "Persistence."

Bart, a fast-talking veteran collector who will be our instructor for the week, reviews the company's history. The collection company was founded many years ago and now has several offices around the country besides this one in the Buffalo, New York, area.

Trevor, a stylishly dressed trainee sitting next to me, yawns widely. Having worked at two other collection companies, he is not easily impressed. He has jumped to this agency in search of easier money. There are literally dozens of collection offices like this one that operate in Buffalo and the surrounding area.

"It's all about the paper," he says, using industry jargon for past-due accounts. At one place where he worked, "the paper hadn't been worked at all yet—these people hadn't been called once."

Not all debts are equal, Trevor explains in a whisper while Bart writes on the board. Some accounts have been "beaten down," or called on by numerous collectors already. Lenders will send their delinquent accounts to one collection agency after another. Each agency sifts out the easier ones, leaving behind the tough nuts. Some accounts have been through three, four, or even five agencies already, and are several years old. The training material in the black binders that we've been issued states that old accounts aren't necessarily harder to collect. People's circumstances might have changed, putting them in a position to pay. Bad luck doesn't last forever. To me, however, this sounds like motivational rhetoric designed to encourage persistence.

Another experienced collector chimes in from behind us. "This place has a good reputation," giving it an inside track with major banks, he says. This is important for getting good-quality accounts. Trevor explains that with good enough accounts and a sharp enough "talk-off"—the spiel used on debtors—a collector can fulfill his monthly goal well before the deadline. This takes the pressure off to make goal. Better yet, it gives you a chance to earn bonus money. The bonus is based on the amount collected above the monthly goal. As the company's brochure promises, "We give you the ability to write your own paycheck," referring to the bonus system. "The harder you work, the more money you will make."

Once Bart has finished the paperwork for our ID badges and the like, our training begins in earnest. Topic number one is the U.S. Fair Debt Collection Practices Act, the consumer protection law that regulates debt collection. Our binders contain the full text of the law, plus page after page of hypothetical situations to illustrate the law's application. There's also an overview of various state laws, which sometimes set higher standards for collectors' conduct than the federal act.

This is impressive. To devote this much attention to consumer protection, beginning on the first day, is not what I expected. However, as we discuss how to apply the rules in hypothetical situations, a subtext to the official lesson becomes clear. Along with learning what the law says, we're also learning how to skirt it.

"Try to sound like a friend," Bart advises. When calling a debtor's home or office, adopt an offhand tone. Call people by their first name—or better yet, their nickname. Ask for Bill or Liz, not William or Elizabeth. Keep up the pretense long enough to get the debtor on the line.

It's an adroit maneuver that flips an important consumer protection on its head. To protect the debtor's privacy, the law forbids revealing the nature of a collection call to "third parties" like housemates or relatives. Collectors are supposed to be vague about the reason for the call until they have the debtor on the line. By taking this vagueness one step further and pretending the call is a personal one, as Brad instructed, we can gain an edge in our cat-and-mouse game with nonpayers.

Another minor deception along those lines is to withhold the name of the company. We're supposed to divulge it only when asked, again as a protection for the debtor's privacy. Brad has a way of turning this restriction to our advantage.

"When someone asks where we are calling from, say 'Buffalo' instead of the company name," he advises. "It's not the answer they're looking for, but they weren't specific. If you can act like a friend for as long as possible, great."

There's also a way to use the "mute" button on our phones to spy on debtors. The button allows us to hear what's being said on the other end of the line, while the debtor hears only flat silence. Thinking they're on hold, they might speak freely to whomever is nearby. We can listen in and glean information about their ability and willingness to pay.

By the time we break for lunch, it is already clear that the business operates with two sets of rules—one to show the outside world and one to live by. As we file out to the break room, the collector with the wireless headset is still on his feet, pacing his aisle of cubicles. He's arguing with a debtor who seems to be asking for more time. "As long as you wait, your credit just gets worse, and worse, and worse," he says, patting the air downward with his hands. It's my first glimpse of the perform-ance aspect of the job, which some skilled collectors raise to an art form.

In the break room, a spiky-haired guy in his twenties describes a run-in he's had with our agency's compliance department. This depart-ment audits a fraction of the calls that are made and enforces adher-ence to our agency's rules as well as debtor protection law. The collector tells us he had left a message stating that, if the debtor didn't return his call that day, he would be forced to "make a decision on their behalf."

"They said I have to stop saying that," he tells the group of us sit-ting at his lunch table.

"What was the decision?" I ask. The guy, who is two or three weeks ahead of me in the training program, stares at me. "The deci-sion you had to make," I ask again. He shrugs and explains that it is just something you say. He faced no penalty beyond the admonition.

The overall thrust of debtor protection law is simple: Don't harass, threaten, or deceive, and don't breach the debtor's privacy. The restrictions that stem from the general prohibitions are many. Don't call before 8:00 a.m. or after 9:00 p.m. Don't communicate by postcard, and on and on.

It takes us three days to get an overview of the federal law, plus a smattering of state laws that add more specific protections. Massachu-setts prohibits taking postdated checks; Vermont, alone in the nation, forbids us to examine its residents' credit reports. Minnesota requires each of us to be individually licensed with its state regulatory office.

Bart emphasizes the exceptions to the rules. We can call after 9:00 p.m., for example, if we have the debtor's permission. We may also call their cell phone, talk to others about their debt, and even take a payment from someone other than the debtor, as long as we have permission. The key is to document the permission in the notes we file with every call. "If you have it documented, the burden of proof is on them," he says. "Most times, our notes will be the only record of what was said during the call," he continues. We get the point.

After three days of instruction, we take a one-page test. I'm relieved when my score comes back perfect, after all my research on collection abuses. Trevor nearly flunks, missing three of the ten questions. He dismisses the result. "All this doesn't mean anything once we get out there," he says. On the collection floor, "it's only about money." Bart goes over the correct answer to each question, and then administers a makeup test on the spot for those who flunked. It's the same test we just took. Everyone passes.

On a Thursday, we receive certificates for completion of classroom training, or "Part One." We take these with our coats, binders, and soda cans to our new desks in the training area. It's a miniature version of the main collection floor, holding several dozen cubicles in two rows. Each stall has a Formica desk flanked by fabric-covered dividers, with an ancient computer terminal and a telephone. We are split up and seated among slightly more experienced people who are a few weeks further along. This group, called "Part Two" training, is performing actual collection work as part of its on-the-job training program.

The stalls exhibit aspects of their occupants' personality, by chance or by design. One woman's desk is littered with empty bags of Cheetos and Evian bottles. Some of the older trainees have tacked up snapshots of their kids to the fabric walls. My space gets the all-business look with photocopies of telephone scripts and computer instructions thumbtacked to the walls. Prominently displayed over the phone is the official script for a phone message, its problematic "mini-Miranda" warning burnished with yellow highlighter. On the desk is a calculator, a notebook for scratch paper on which to write the reference numbers of hot prospects, and the binder of training materials with red and yellow page tabs at important sections.

The office itself is almost entirely without decoration. By the elevators are a couple of framed pictures that look as though they came from the same place as the desks and filing cabinets. It's clear that these touches are for visiting clients, like the ficus in its brass stand. The walls above our cubes are adorned by simple banners, white with a gold border, that trumpet the company's collection prowess. Each one exclaims how in a particular month the goal was some number of dollars, and the amount collected a somewhat larger figure. The dates go back to 2001. The usual rate seems to be about $2 million in monthly revenue, up from $1.5 million in 2001.

At the head of our training group, at the end of our two rows of cubes, stands a dry-erase whiteboard. It displays three columns of figures in green, red, and blue ink. Having obtained a payment, a collector goes to the board and writes the amount, the account number, and his initials. Blue ink is for future payments, such as postdated checks. Red signifies an overnight payment, such as a bank check or money order that will land in the FedEx drop in the morning. Green means cash—money today—usually a check-by-phone with today's date. The board shows at a glance how much money the training group has pulled in, and who is contributing.

Joe, the trainee across the row from me, is hard at work when I take my new seat.

"Ethel, listen to me!" he shouts into his phone. "You did this. YOU did this!"

It sounds like a retired woman on the other end of the line is trying to deny responsibility for a charge account that has been run up in her name. Joe browbeats her for several minutes, rejecting her excuses.

Finally, she hangs up without paying, and he slams down his phone. Gabe, our training group manager, swivels in his chair and publicly chides him for failing to get payment. Joe complains that the debtor was a hard case.

"That's why I gave you the account," Gabe replies.

I wonder why Joe dismissed the woman's denial. Identity theft is real, after all. I will soon learn that collectors hear the excuse so often that they're not easily taken in by it. Claiming ignorance of the debt is often a debtor's first line of defense. A quick check of the account record will tell whether the claim is supported or not. If the account was immediately maxed out and then closed for nonpayment, the circumstances point to ID theft—especially if the account address is inconsistent with those on the debtor's credit report. But if the account was open for months or years, with bills going to the debtor's known address, theft seems unlikely. "Someone made payments on that account; thieves don't make payments," collectors argue.

By hitting a two-key sequence, I pull up an account onto my screen and go to work. On this day, we're working a batch of accounts from a major credit card issuer. The main screen shows the debtor's name, primary and secondary phone numbers, the notes from recent call attempts, and a summary of the supposed debt—name of the creditor and how much is left unpaid. We are told to work the order of business: Get the debtor on the phone, demand payment, and rebut their excuses. If they won't pay in full, offer a settlement, starting high and working down. As a last resort, set up a monthly payment plan, starting with a down payment of at least 10 percent of the balance. It sounds simple, but we'll learn the art of rebuttals later, when we are tutored by collection pros on the floor.

For the rest of the day, I make call after call but do not reach a single debtor, at least not one who admits being a debtor. "Jason is in the hospital," a man says when I ask for the person whose name is on the account, using the friendly first-name ploy. "This is his father, I'm his guardian. He's been in the hospital since November—hit by a car—he's not right in the head." After hanging up, I look at the account record more carefully and realize that Jason must be in his 50s, going by his date of birth. Probably it was the guy who answered the phone, making up a story designed to get me to stop calling.

The fact that debtors are running deceptions on us all the time helps my coworkers rationalize the scams we run on them. Other trainees just a few weeks out of Brad's classroom readily share the tricks they've learned as we finish out the week.

For example, when offering a settlement, you might pretend to be filling out an application. Blandly ask the debtor for their work address and phone number, their spouse's work number, and annual income. You act bored as you fill in blanks on a routine form. In reality, there's not an application; it's a ruse to get more information for your own use. The settlement rates are preapproved. The additional facts and phone numbers could be useful later in the collection process. We must fill in the blanks on this screen before the computer will accept a settlement, so we broadly construe this as an application. If the settlement offer falls through, or the debtor stops making payments, it will be that much harder for them to avoid our calls. As the mini-Miranda warning states, any information we obtain will be used for the purpose of collecting a debt.

The sheets thumbtacked to my cube are full of instructions for quick reference. One sheet lists the standard abbreviations used in our notes on each account to describe common situations. OTB means "out to borrow," what we say in our account notes when we've convinced someone to pay their bill by borrowing from friends or relatives, or from a loan company—even from the equity in their home. NLE stands for "no longer employed," a common excuse for nonpayment. Our response is to ask about their unemployment benefits. If they say their benefits only cover basic expenses, we demand to know why they are paying these other bills, and not the one we are seeking. PTP means "promise to pay," meaning the debtor will be able to pay at a future date. Seen nearly as often as PTP is its corollary, PBK, which stands for "promise broken." PIF stands for "Payment in Full," the collector's Holy Grail, payment of the full balance due on the account. A more realistic goal is to shoot for SIF, "settlement in full."

Sometimes, a nonpayer will offer an array of excuses: Their job ended, their health failed, their spouse left, their car exploded, their house burned down, or the dog died. It might be necessary to listen to these tales of woe, but there is no need to repeat them in our notes. A three-letter code covers it all: HLS stands for "hard-luck story."

The other sheets worthy of being thumbtacked to my cube are scripts for calls. One is for messages left on an answering machine.

Another is for speaking with someone who knows the debtor. Almost all the calls we make terminate in an answering machine, if there's any response at all. The machine script contains the sentence that we call the mini-Miranda warning. "This call is an attempt to collect a debt, and any information obtained will be used for that purpose." We are to state that in messages to the debtor's primary phone number on the account, and when speaking to a debtor, our training says.

"You don't have to say that," says Aaron, the collector to my right, after overhearing me recite the mini-Miranda into the phone for a few days. Aaron is no Joe. He uses a soft-voiced, friendly approach that emphasizes the benefits of settling the account. But he's no fool, either. No one, or practically no one, repeats the long and boring disclosure statement, though most of us have tacked it up in our cubicle. Joe shows me the message he really uses, handwritten on a scrap of notebook paper he can slide under his keyboard. It's a variation on the ominous "decision on your behalf" message that was supposedly outlawed by compliance.

Three training managers patrol our end of the room. They jump on the phone when we get a live debtor to provide a "second voice" and show us how to record payments on the computer system—something we get little practice with. The training managers also assiduously avoid acknowledging breaches of the official process. At one point, Joe asks Mabel, the training group manager, to look at the message he has worked up—he seems proud of it—and she refuses. "We gave you the message [script]," she tells him. "If you're using something else, I don't want to know about it."

The computers here are no newer than the antiques back in the classroom. Small, black-and-white screens that display only text, they are throwbacks to the days before Microsoft invented Windows. A cursor blinks on a black background, awaiting a command from one of the lists thumbtacked on my wall. The advanced age of these little tubes belies their power, however. They can reach into the tens of thousands of account records, which are stored in servers stacked somewhere in the depths of the building. They can pull up screen after screen of information on each of these thousands of accounts. Another program taps an online database that can find current and old addresses as well as phone numbers at work and home; it can even search for the debtor's relatives and neighbors, based on surname and address.

The most powerful tool, however, is the credit report, which pops on the screen instantly from one of the major credit bureaus. The credit report lists your debts, paid and unpaid, and your open charge accounts, plus bankruptcies and civil judgments. To a trained eye, it lays bare your financial pressure points. A mortgage payment means there's a house you might lose. A big car payment means you have a ride that you're proud of. To a collector, possessions equal weakness.

Even with all the tricks in the book, getting money from people who don't want to pay is a frustrating task. It takes persistence, all right. Toward the end of the day, Benjamin, a gentle-voiced collector on my row says, "If one more person hangs up on me, I'm going to snap."

"What do they think," his buddy Aaron replies, "the money is just free?"

Even though I've just started, I don't remember having ever been so glad for the passage of time on a Friday afternoon, as the clock ticks toward 5:00 p.m. to end my first week as a collector.

Action Item: Stop Collection Calls

Under the Fair Debt Collection Practices Act, you may demand that a collection agency stop contacting you. The cease communication demand must be made in writing and should be sent by certified mail. Upon receiving your letter, the agency may contact you only to confirm that it has stopped collection efforts, or to advise you that it is pursuing other remedies to obtain payment. For more on this aspect of the FDCPA, see Chapter 22, "Using Collection Law."

2

Credit Is King

My cheap desk, in a nondescript call center, provides a frontline view of an enormous economic battleground. On one side are the banks and other creditors that send us past-due accounts. Arrayed against them are consumers, or "debtors" as we call them, whether or not they actually owe money. These are the people who have signed up for the buy-now-pay-later philosophy that used to keep the U.S. economy rolling.

We have known for years that the nation is addicted to debt, but shelved the uncomfortable fact and kept on spending. Now the bill has come due. The financial crisis of 2008 has hit, followed by the great payback of 2009—and 2010, 2011, and so on. It will take years to pay down debts that were racked up during the binge. With a deep recession causing more and more bills to go unpaid, my collector colleagues are rolling up their sleeves and getting to work in earnest. In 2009, more consumers fell behind on their loan payments than at any time since the banking industry started recording consumer delinquencies in 1974.[1] Some estimates say as much as $186 billion in bank credit card balances will go bad by the end of 2010.[2]

When creditors tire of trying to collect delinquent balances themselves, they outsource the job to a professional collection agency. The agency can escalate the effort, whereas the original creditor distances itself from the tougher tactics that are used. Creditors send us all kinds of bills. Bounced checks, ATM overdrafts, store accounts from Home Depot to Neiman Marcus, and special-purpose loans for the kind of merchandise that is hawked on late-night infomercials. There are auto loan "deficiencies," or the amount still due after the car has been towed back to the lot. Some of the debts are loans that people received from their tax preparer, thinking it was their tax refund in advance. But, by far, the majority of the accounts we see are for general-purpose credit cards—Visa, MasterCard, and the others to a lesser extent—from issuers big and small across the country.

Plastic is the American consumer's best friend and worst enemy. It's a magic wand for consumption. Wave it, and you have the spending power you haven't yet earned. Load up on luxuries like a new pair of skis or an exotic vacation. Or just get necessities like a load of groceries and a tank of gas. Do this enough and the balance climbs to the limit, while the monthly payments become a choking burden. The gas is used up, the groceries are long gone, but the payments last and last. If you make only minimum monthly payments, you'll be paying off that load of groceries for years. It does not require a big balance or a luxurious lifestyle to run up high interest charges. By the time you finally erase a $1,000 balance, you will have paid twice that much in interest, at the interest rate and minimum monthly repayment rate that is typical on most cards.

"Cash is king," the saying goes. But those days are long gone. Credit is the reigning sovereign of economic life. In the years since BankAmericard, now Visa, launched the first general-purpose credit card with a revolving balance in 1959, consumer credit has spread to every corner of the economy. The average home has three open credit card accounts. Nearly half of all Americans carry a balance on their cards, with the average household's balance being over $7,000.[3] Furthermore, the amount you can borrow on each of those cards is rising fast—or at least it was, until recently.

Credit was almost as easy to get as it is to use—as anyone with a mailbox full of offers from credit card issuers can attest. In recent years, banks thought it was a good idea to keep boosting people's credit limits, reaching an average of $18,000 per family in 2007.

Three out of four households have at least one credit card, up from half of households in 1970. People who needed a parent to cosign their first credit card application are surprised to see their own children being tempted with preapproved credit offers before they graduate from college.

Credit cards are by no means the only source of consumers' debt load, or even the largest source. Home mortgages constitute the heaviest burden on family budgets, followed by school loans, according to the Federal Reserve. The typical family spends 18 percent of its income paying off debts, a fraction that has risen with increases in the price of homes and college tuition. As a nation, consumers are indebted to the tune of $13 trillion,[4] a sum greater than the combined economic output of Japan, Germany, and Canada. Of that amount, credit cards, car loans, and other supposedly short-term obligations make up $2 trillion, according to the Federal Reserve, a figure that has nearly doubled in ten years. Debt from credit cards alone amounts to about $900 billion.[5] Americans are drowning in debt, concludes the Center for American Progress. Hefty home loans have contributed to a swelling debt load for typical middle-class families, the liberal think tank said in a 2006 report.[6]

Yet not everyone is drowning. In fact, some consumers are serenely floating on debt's surface. Of families that have a credit card, a little more than half are able to pay off their entire bill each month. By not carrying a balance, they benefit from interest-free loans during the grace period in their billing cycle. They enjoy the convenience of booking hotels and airline tickets with plastic. They can make online purchases of everything from cars to books and cell-phone airtime, without paying interest or transaction fees. It is the other 46 percent of consumers who pick up the tab, in the form of interest rates averaging 13 percent (them, plus merchants who are charged a fee on each transaction). Those families that can scrape together only enough to make the monthly minimum payment are helping pay for the purchasing convenience that others enjoy. According to a GAO report issued in 2006, credit card issuers generate 10 percent of their profits from late fees.[7]

Finally, the effects of the debt binge have become impossible to ignore. At about the time that I went to work for the agency, headlines began to appear about the home mortgage crisis. Overextended home buyers started reneging on their outsized mortgage payments in large numbers. This was alarming when you consider how lenders had justified the high interest loans in the first place: To pay their mortgage, people do whatever it takes, according to the conventional wisdom. Families scrimp and sacrifice to keep the roof over their heads. So, what does it mean when large numbers of homeowners no longer pay the single, most important bill they face?

Now, of course, we know the answer to that question. The consumption binge is over and the long, slow process of paying off the bills has begun. Sure enough, defaults on debts other than home mortgages have shot up. Car loans, retail credit, and general credit cards, those wonderful tools for everyday living, are going unpaid. Near the end of 2009, credit card delinquencies measured by ratings services like Fitch Ratings were hovering around record highs they had set in the summer. About one in every 20 credit card accounts was more than 30 days late with a payment.[8]

That is where the professional debt collector comes in. Alongside the phenomenon of easy credit has grown an industry that is not so easygoing. There are about 434,000 people in the United States collecting unpaid debts on behalf of creditors like banks, utilities, insurers, retail stores, and government offices, according to the U.S. Bureau of Labor Statistics.[9] Of these debt collectors, about 108,000 work in professional or "third-party" collection agencies like my employer. The majority are "in-house" collectors, who work directly for creditors such as utilities, hospitals, and banks. Even though they are fewer in number, third-party collectors generate three times as many FTC complaints as in-house collectors.[10]

Third-party agencies are contractors. They're hired by creditors to bring in money that the creditor was unable to collect through its own efforts. This army of professional collection workers is expected to swell, now that the consumer debt bubble has burst: The Bureau of Labor Statistics predicts that about 100,000 new collection jobs will be created in the decade that ends in 2016, a "much faster" growth rate than average for all occupations.[11]

Collection agencies are powerfully motivated by the contingency fee system that awards them a fraction of what they collect. The fee ranges between about 10 cents to 50 cents of each dollar collected. The size of the fee corresponds with the age of the accounts. The older they are, the more collectors have already tried—and failed—to wring money from them. This might be the account's second, third, fourth, or even fifth time around. In 2005, the industry recovered nearly $40 billion to businesses, the industry trade association ACA International estimates.[12] NCO Group, the Philadelphia-area holding company that is ranked as the nation's largest collector, reported $1.4 billion in U.S. revenue for 2008.[13] Like the invention of credit card debt, the job of collecting money on behalf of someone else is a relatively recent phenomenon—as a legitimate business, at least. There have always been thugs who accompanied a bookie or a loan shark, or worked on his behalf. The title character in the original *Rocky* movie worked as one of these loan shark collectors before he found a different outlet for his skills. This breed of third-party collectors probably got their start collecting shells and beads. Historians think the practice of lending dates back to the beginnings of agriculture, and with lending came collecting.[14] Efforts to rein in collectors' zeal extend back into antiquity. Mesopotamia's legal code included a section that forbade lenders from seizing farmers' grain after a poor harvest. The proscription seemed intended to keep a bad year from degenerating into famine. There's no record of how well the lenders followed the rules.

These days, the professional collection establishment in the United States works hard to distinguish itself from the older, unsavory side of the collection business. The American Collectors Association, now called ACA International, set up shop in 1939 to set standards for collectors' conduct. It also strives to put a professional face on the industry—a different face than the glowering, bent-nosed one in the popular imagination. In the 1970s, ACA supported a federal consumer protection law that barred debt collectors from using harassment, intimidation, and false threats as tools of their trade. The group also polices its membership and looks into complaints of harsh tactics. A modern, professional collection agency recognizes that harassment is ineffective as well as illegal, ACA tells us. Instead of alienating consumers, collectors are trained to help them find ways to pay their bills and get out of debt, according to the industry group.

But not all the estimated 4,300 or more collection agencies in the United States are members of ACA, and not all live up to its standards. Agencies that need a spotless image have the most incentive to adhere to the professional ideals. Those that collect on behalf of government agencies or image-conscious banks, for example, risk getting fired by their clients if complaints about threats and harassment grow too loud. These agencies represent one end of a spectrum that stretches across a broad range of ethical and legal boundaries.

Banks, utilities, hospitals, and other big companies support the third-party collection system in two ways. First, they farm out debts to agencies, like the one where I worked, on a contract basis. The agency earns a cut of whatever it collects. This contingency work used to be the mainstay of the collection industry, but it is giving way to another market that is less controlled. Lenders are selling off their bad debts on a wide-open market to anyone who can pay. For a small percentage of the debt's face amount, a broker, debt buyer, or collection company can obtain large numbers of accounts. On this market, debts typically cost only 5 percent of the balance due, according to one estimate from a Federal Reserve economist.[15] The oldest debts can be had for less than 2 percent of the balance.

In Minnesota, home of some major collection operations, a wave of abuses has caught the attention of the state's consumer watchdog agencies. Minnesota has some of the nation's tightest restrictions on collectors and some of the most rigorous enforcement, making it an early warning indicator of collection industry abuses. Back in 2004, officials sounded an alarm about a new level of shakedown that goes beyond forbidden harassment techniques. "We are now seeing companies...crossing the line by trying to coerce consumers into paying unsubstantiated debts and amounts that were not even owed by them in the first place," the state's attorney general said in a public announcement.[16] The occasion for that zinger was the office's filing of lawsuits against two aggressive collectors.

Consumer advocates believe that ruthless intimidation tactics are spreading within the industry like a virus. The industry disputes this and says complaints by consumers are a natural part of their business. But the economic pressures for tough tactics to spread are clear. The accounts that pop up on my screen, like Samantha's, have come to my agency because our client expects a healthy return on its money. If harder-edged agencies are more successful, the accounts will likely go to them instead. With a wide-open market for debt sales, accounts from the biggest banks can wind up anywhere, including in the hands of scam operators with extortionate tactics.

Action Item: Disputing a Supposed Debt

To dispute a debt or a portion of it, send a certified letter to the collection agency putting forth your argument within 30 days of being contacted. To continue collection efforts, the agency is required to provide you with verification of the debt, under the U.S. Fair Debt Collection Practices Act. Disputing a debt might halt collection efforts; but if not, it is an important step to have covered. See Chapters 22, 23, and 24, ("Using Collection Law," "Reading Your Credit Reports," and "Preparing a Complaint," respectively) for more information on disputing a debt.

3

Anger Can Be Power

On my commute to begin my second week as a collector, a pickup truck cuts me off. My ears burn and my shoulders tense. With difficulty, I stifle the urge to blast my horn at the offender. As my blood cools, an idea forms: Anger is a resource that the tough collectors—guys like Joe—channel into their work. Their mood seems set on a hair-trigger release for indignation. Maybe I can prime myself the same way, to be prepared to argue with debtors, instead of being caught flat-footed and letting them get the upper hand. I have those same aggressive impulses that are inappropriate for everyday life, unless you enjoy bar fights and road-rage encounters.

Then I do a double take. What am I thinking? Having learned to rein in my caveman impulses, I should now learn to unleash them? To the contrary, over the weekend I had come up with a plan to survive in the job, or at least make it through training, without becoming another Joe. Instead of adopting the tough tone and tactics, I'll sweet-talk them over to my side—stressing the benefits of cooperation, hinting at the settlement that can knock off a chunk of the debt. Some of these balances can be knocked down by 50 percent, the steep discount that's already preapproved by the creditor.

So, at my desk I write out a new script for messages—an important tool because almost all the speaking I do is with answering machines. "I've reviewed your file and I think we can get this resolved," the block letters state. All they have to do is come up with the settlement amount. "I look forward to working with you on this," my script ends.

I crank through my calls with this until the batch of accounts we are working runs out. I stick my head up and ask if there's a new batch. Training managers walk through periodically and announce a new code for us to punch into our machines to enter a new trove of accounts. In our company, as in most of the industry, this is called a WIP, for "work in progress." It might contain hundreds or thousands of accounts. Floor collectors have their own WIPs to work. As trainees, we share. There's usually an East Coast WIP to start the day. We can begin calling people in our time zone right away at 8:00 a.m. By 9:00 a.m., there's a batch of Central Time Zone accounts, as the morning rolls westward across the country. At 11:00 a.m., we eagerly begin calling California and the other western states, where it is still early enough to perhaps catch people before they leave for work. The hours 8:00 a.m. to 10:00 a.m. and 5:00 p.m. to 8:00 p.m. are deemed "prime time," the best hours for reaching people at home. The dead zone in between is the time to "skip-trace" accounts, or track down a debtor whose phone and address information is out of date. Like many others, this agency subscribes to an online database service called Accurint for this purpose. It's capable of searching by name, address, or Social Security number. However, it's not a magic lamp. Usually, if the number on the credit report is old, Accurint will have no further information. The real work of skip-tracing involves picking up the phone and cajoling the debtor's old neighbors, landlord, or coworkers for their new address or phone number. Collectors can use these permissible calls to neighbors and work places as a potential pressure tactic as well, if word gets back to the debtor about them.

Joe pops up on the other side of the divider between our cubes. With the WIP empty, now is the time to work on the accounts in your desk, he says. "Do you have any accounts in your desk?" I'm not even sure what he means by my desk, so my answer is "no."

"Why not?" he says, with the tone of voice I've heard him use on the phone with debtors. Bart's teaching failed to cover some basics that he expected us to pick up on our own. The training method here is the sink-or-swim approach.

Joe explains that each day we can put six accounts in our "desk," which is the term for a digital space reserved for my use in the computer system. Hot prospects in your desk, such as those who have promised a future payment, can't be worked by other collectors. "You should always, always keep them," he says, in his authoritative tone. "Keep working them to keep them there. That means a touch every day—a new note, something." A touch would be opening the account record and noting that a call was attempted.

I'm uncomfortable that Joe is tutoring me, taking me under his wing. He'd noted with approval earlier that my shoulder was to the wheel, listening to me make call after futile call. After he explains how to save accounts in my desk, he advises me how to work them. He pulls a scrap of notebook paper from under his keyboard, the special call script that he has worked up. It's a brazenly illegal string of implied threats, laced with warnings not to ignore his call. I seize an excuse to return to my desk, not wanting to have to pretend gratitude.

We are scheduled to work two evening shifts a week, in order to call debtors after their workday. On the first of these evening shifts, Joe is working at full blast, despite the hour, telling jokes when he's not talking to a debtor. At one point, he adopts a Sylvester-the-cat lisp to leave a message. "I call her every day," he said to the group, laughing, after he hung up. The recipient was someone who had reneged on a promise to pay.

Later, he adopts a broadly fake accent when pretending to be on the phone with a Spanish-speaking debtor. Hispanics often stymie collectors by claiming not to know English, making them the target of particular resentment in my office. Collectors suspect that these debtors are hiding behind a false language barrier. "Speak English!" my coworkers will bark. Officially, we're supposed to transfer them to a Spanish-speaking department, if the debtor can't or won't get one of their bilingual family members on the line to translate. But it rubs collectors against the grain to let go of a live debtor.

At my end of the row of cubicles, there's a loosely defined group of trainees who, as time goes on, talk and joke together more and more, and share tricks they've learned. If we were in an old war movie, Joe would be the sly schemer who wins the poker games and has some scam cooking with the quartermaster. Bobby, a young guy whose overgelled hair sticks up in shiny spikes, is the wise-cracking bon vivant who always has a word for the mademoiselles. His buddy Aaron would be the medic, whose wry humor overlays a deep vein of warmth. Benjamin, on my right, is the pudgy greenhorn that you worry about—he seems too soft to become a warrior. The cube to my left is vacant at first, but is soon filled—almost literally filled to the edges—when Bart's next group of trainees pass their tests and take their seats among us.

The commander is Mabel, the training group manager, a lean, hardened veteran who can deliver glowing approval or a reprimand with merely a glance. Her lieutenants, Gabe and Julie, are less remote, more ready to pitch in with us troops on a workaday task like taking a payment.

I suppose my role is that of the bookish, bespectacled foot soldier who doesn't talk much. Hopefully, I'm not one of the expendable characters who gets written out of the story in the first few scenes, before the squad fights its way off the landing beach. The rapid ups and downs of the work make it seem like anything can happen, especially considering our lack of experience. Every time we make a call, it is like taking a step in a minefield.

Bobby recounts an unnerving call. The account record had the guy's name and Social Security number right, but the address didn't match the one in Accurint. In fact, it didn't match any address where the debtor had ever lived. "It's fraud," Bobby says, on his way to tell Gabe. "Someone else must've signed up for the card."

"You know what I'd do about it: period, enter," Joe says. The key-strokes period-enter close the account on your screen, burying it back in the work-in-progress queue to be dealt with on some other day by another collector. I see his point. Bobby has already burned through precious minutes with this "debtor." It will take even more time to straighten out the situation so that the account can be pulled from the queue. There's no incentive for correcting an account that is in error. To the contrary, every minute spent clearing up a false or fraudulent bill is a minute wasted, from the perspective of making our quotas and keeping our jobs.

Even being a fraud victim doesn't necessarily let people off the hook. One debtor tells Benjamin that her daughter must've run up the charges. The mother claimed she hadn't used the credit card, and was unaware of the bill until his call. Ben gave up on her, but Gabe told him to call the mom back. His advice: Tell the mom to file a police report on the daughter. Otherwise, it's still her obligation to pay. "She's scamming you," Gabe said. "You can't have it both ways." If a stranger ran up bills on your card, you wouldn't hesitate to bring in the law. Just because the culprit turns out to be your offspring doesn't mean the debt is erased. We get tough with the mom, she gets tough with the daughter, and the bill gets paid. At least, that is how Gabe sees it. But I could tell that Benjamin was having trouble carrying out those instructions. He eventually said he was unable to get the woman on the phone again.

Behind us, the windows that line the office are covered with thin blinds that filter the daylight and block the view, as if the sight of the parking lot or the stucco-walled building next door would distract us. Tethered to our phones, eyes focused on our screens, we are in an eight-hour isolation tank from the outside world. At home in the evening, I'm ambushed by news stories that I am amazed to have missed during the day. Alarming signs of economic misery are piling up. Mortgage defaults are leaping to record levels and more and more homes are plunging into foreclosure. Layoffs are surging. One radio report said that some cities are seeing more bankruptcy filings than marriages.

My coworkers aren't much for talking about current events, but even in our dim office fenced into cubes, we can see the onset of a very difficult time for people with debt. There are more debtors in trouble, which means more accounts to work for collectors like us. But the debtors will have less money, so it will be even harder to squeeze anything out of them. What with jobs ebbing and prices going up for gas, food, and everything else, who will have spare money to make payments on their old debts?

The one piece of news that is discussed widely in the building is the coming stimulus payments that will put checks of $600 or more into people's mailboxes. Collectors smell opportunity. "I've gotta work that into my talk-off," one older collector tells me in the break room. Those checks give us another rebuttal. You say you have no money to pay your bill? What about your stimulus check! This might not be how the Council of Economic Advisers envisioned the money would be spent, and it's not clear how paying years-old credit card bills, laden with penalties and interest, will stimulate the economy— at least the larger economy. It will certainly put a smile on the face of bankers, and their hirelings at collection agencies.

At midweek, having made about 250 phone calls since the end of classroom training, I collect my first payment. The amount is all of $212.66 from an elderly lady in Philadelphia, the unpaid balance on a Sears card. I called her number once, talked to her sister, then called back later at the time I had been told, and the debtor actually came to the phone.

"It's really not much of a balance, maybe we could just take care of it today," I say blandly, appealing to her pride. "It must have just been an oversight."

Her smooth voice and proper diction suggest a churchy matron. I picture her sitting at a telephone table with a doily under the black dial phone. Certainly, she agrees, she has that much in checking. She'll just go ahead and pay the bill.

I nearly choke. "Well, I can take your check over the phone ma'am, and save you a trip to the mailbox." She agrees to that as well, reading me the digits at the bottom of her check, the routing number and account number that we need to process a check by phone. My kill-them-with-kindness routine worked. And why not—who would give their bank account number to a rude stranger? But I wonder at her readiness to pay. She doesn't remember the bill, but takes my word that she owes it. She even has to wait while I struggle to use the payment screens. I flag down Gabe to help me, having had no practice with this part of the job. Eventually, I have to call her back and transfer her to the authorization department, which audiotapes the debtor's permission for us to draw up the check on their account.

Then it is time to note the score on the whiteboard. "Does a check for today count as green?" I ask Mabel with mock innocence.

"Give it up, y'all," she says.

My first payment. "That's the hard one, right?" A brief applause rises from the cubicles. "Woo," I say, uncapping the marker, "this green ink smells good."

It's a relatively tiny balance, carrying a fee to the agency of about $50. Still, it's my first score. Until now, it was not clear that I could collect a single dollar. It's the middle of my second week, eighth day of employment, fourth out of the classroom, persistently dialing the phone. It will take another $2,450 in "fee" to the company to survive training and graduate to the floor. At quitting time, I thank Gabe for handling the mechanics of taking the payment and apologize for my lack of practice. Not to worry, he responds. We're not expected to generate big bucks right out of the gate, while we're still learning the computer system and talking to our first debtors.

"I'll tell you some stuff," he says, leaning over the divider. "You can say, 'I just got your personal information faxed to me, including your Social Security number,'" he says. "It's all legal, because you do have their information."

"Slick," I say, feeling uncomfortable.

Telling the story to a friend after work, I realize that I'm unduly proud of my small success. After all, my real goal is to survive the training period, not to become a swaggeringly successful debt collector. For one thing, I need to reach out of my training room circle to make contact with the big hitters on the floor, people in that million-dollar club that the company newsletter applauds. How do they do it, I'd like to know?

The next day is bitter. A fierce windstorm shoves my car around the highway and makes the 20-degree temperature seem even colder. Still, people march outside for their cigarettes during our morning and afternoon breaks, complaining that it takes them the entire 15 minutes just to get one lit. Having given up cigarettes years ago, I spend the break drinking coffee from a vending machine and wishing I had a newspaper, or Internet access.

Midwinter is a good time of year to get a job in the collection industry. Agencies all over the country are gearing up for spring, which means one thing to a collector: tax refunds. Starting in February and continuing for a few months, tapped-out debtors will be receiving a bit of extra cash—tax refunds, earned income credit, refund anticipation loans—and agencies want to be fully prepared to extract it from them.

Even so, I was concerned that agencies would turn me away. I feared that my previous employment as a newspaper reporter, fully listed on my résumé, would raise eyebrows and lead to the discovery of my critical stories about collections. When the interviewer asked why I wanted this job, I told her the truth: that I had heard a lot about collections and wanted to see for myself what it was really like. I got the job offer less than a week later—my background apparently failed to set off alarms in the personnel office. There's no indication that anyone here has ever read a story of mine. Now my earlier concerns seem silly. It is clear that management views me no differently than the other $10-an-hour trainees. What gets attention here is ability. Trevor and one other trainee in my class got an automatic pass to the floor, on the basis of their prior experience and gung-ho attitudes. Once, when Bart asked the room in general if anyone spoke Spanish, Trevor said into the silence, "Well, I speak debtor."

Periodically, we're herded back into the classroom for an hour of further training in finer points that Bart didn't get to. The break from the phone and computer screen is welcome, yet the other guys grumble at the waste of time, acting eager to graduate training so they can start earning bonuses. Mabel tells us that she, before she became training manager, was a consistent collector. For years, she generated $10,000 in monthly "fee." "I wasn't in the million-dollar club, which they have out there," she said, "but I was steady because I was persistent. I had a pace." Pick up the phone, try your hardest to get the money, and then repeat. Two-hundred times a day.

Joe the clown was absent, another small comfort. He had an appointment in the morning, and then failed to come in at noon as planned. He got chewed out over the phone by Gabe. Ben, sitting next to me, hoped aloud that Joe would be fired. "It's so quiet today with Joe out," he said wistfully. I feel a bit sorry for the little monster. He has an ex-wife somewhere, and kids who depended on him. He acts nonchalant about the prospect of being fired, but that could be false bravado. I don't know how badly he needs the job. But you have to figure that anyone willing to do the work we are doing, for the pay that we earn, does not have many other options.

Action Item: Stop Calls at Work

Collectors may call you at work. However, the FDCPA prohibits calls at your place of employment if the collector "knows or has reason to know" that your employer prohibits these calls. Collectors should stop contacting you at work if you tell them that your employer restricts non-work-related calls. For more on this topic, see Chapter 22, "Using Collection Law."

4

Closeout: "No Tomorrow"

On the last business day of the month, Julie calls us to the front of the room for the before-work huddle. Behind her stands the whiteboard where we display the day's payments. Today, it's different. Usually, there are three columns: one, in green ink, for payments that are booked immediately; another, in red ink, for next-day payments coming by overnight mail; and a third, in blue ink, for postdated checks. But today, the three column headings are all in green.

"What is today?" Julie bellows.

"Closeout," we mumble back.

"That's right," she says. "Closeout. End of the month. On the board, there's only money for today." Our instructions are to extract something from the debtor today—period. Promises for future payments will not be entertained. They will not qualify as keepers that we can put in our desk. Next-day payments will not go on the board. "There is no tomorrow," she says.

She hands us ammunition as well to help complete this mission: The major credit card issuer whose accounts we are working has preapproved a settlement rate of 70 percent off the full balance, good for today only. People trot back to their desks with vigor.

With the deadline looming, all efforts focus on bringing in money by the end of the day, as opposed to tracking down deadbeat skip artists or setting up piecemeal, long-term payment plans. But the "no-tomorrow" maxim could have another, harsher meaning as well. For collectors who are short of their monthly goal, time is running out. Even graduates of the training program remain on probation in this respect. If they miss the goal by too much, too often, they can expect to be dismissed. Similarly, managers are evaluated monthly on the collection performance of their group, measured in dollars.

So, closeout, the last business day of the month, ratchets up the pressure throughout the building. Not surprisingly, the people on the other end of the phones feel it as well. With a do-or-die atmosphere saturating the office, harsh tactics that are heard infrequently at other times become loud and common. As the day wears on, I see why telephone offices like this are called "boiler rooms."

"Put Juan on the phone, NOW!" shouts a trainee at the other end of the room, cutting through the din. "Hanging up will just make this a lot worse," someone else warns darkly. When I look up from my screen, I half expect to see the air tinted red by a visible cloud of anger. Bobby works standing up to keep his blood moving. Over the divider, I hear him identify himself as a fraud investigator, looking into suspicious activity on a credit card. That's a novel and brazenly illegal trick. It combines misrepresentation and an implied threat of legal action, maybe even criminal prosecution, all rolled into one false statement. I remember hearing this ploy before, on a tape supplied by Idaho's consumer protection office. They had obtained it from the answering machine of a resident who was complaining of harassment by a different collection agency. So the fraud-investigator ploy isn't original with Bobby—more like it's a tactic that has been passed around among collectors.

None of us, except the newest recruit right out of the classroom, repeats the boilerplate disclosure statements that we are technically supposed to say. The disclosure statement that we call the mini-Miranda, which is included prominently in our training binder, informs the debtor that our call is an attempt to collect a debt, and any information obtained will be used for that purpose. The disclosure is required by the Fair Debt Collection Practices Act on the first contact with a consumer; indeed, the language is almost a verbatim quote from the text of the law. But no message with such a statement would be returned, and we would be talking fruitlessly into our phones until we are hoarse.

Managers hear us omitting these statements and using very different language than the approved message script, but they say nothing about it. So, while everyone ignores the mini-Miranda disclosure rule, the company can claim that it is their policy to make disclosure on every call. It's written right there in the training manual, and the script is provided to each and every collector.

The compliance department must know that we are not using the warning, if they are indeed auditing some of our calls. But I see no crackdown. In fact, I only heard of one instance where compliance chewed someone out during my entire tenure at the agency. At first, I assume this is because the department does not push too hard on minor issues like boilerplate disclosure statements. Later on, I will learn the truth about the compliance department's role.

Certainly, the managers working among us are not reining in anyone's behavior. Bobby's "talk-off" is brazenly illegal and he is not at all discrete about making his threats of criminal prosecution. If Bobby were fired for his infractions, the company would be sending a strong message about compliance. It would also lose the most capable collector in the training group.

Across from me, Joe is uncharacteristically soft-voiced. He is calling, not the general accounts in the work in progress (WIP), but his follow-ups, people in his desk who have made some sort of promise to pay. To them, he's offering the 70 percent off settlement, hoping it will prod them into action.

I make call after call. Deep down though, I am hoping that there's no answer, so I don't have to confront a debtor—not with the sketchy information that is available to me on the account records. We are working a difficult batch of credit card accounts. They're so old, the home phone numbers are usually wrong. If the number works at all, it is usually answered by someone who has inherited the debtor's number. They are sick of getting collection calls. An address search and reverse phone number search can be used to check their story, but the results are often inconclusive. At midmorning, Mabel announces that collectors who post a same-day payment will get a $10 gas card. "Gosh, I'm motivated enough already," I say to Aaron. "Keep the gas card and give me some halfway decent accounts."

At the end of the week, the class behind us files out of the training room, ready to work the phones. The empty stall next to mine is filled with a booming voice and a broad back that almost seems wedged between the dividers. "Hello! This is Gary Nardozzi!" my new coworker bellows into his phone. He's loud enough to drown out my voice in the next carrel, so I am forced to nearly shout as well.

Gary starts having success on the phone right away. His simple and direct approach works. His plain, blunt manner makes him seem trustworthy, keeping his robust friendliness from seeming excessive or forced. Collectors have different styles that tend to work on different people. The style I'm developing is a businesslike approach. My speech is correct and somewhat formal, conveying respect and, I hope, integrity. You will get no verbal backslapping from me, just straight talk. "This is just business," I say quietly when someone becomes irate. "There's nothing personal here, no reason to get emotional." Gary's style is the opposite. Somehow, he forms a human connection before he even reveals what he's calling about. His booming "hello, glad I got 'hold of you!" is like an arm over the shoulder— friendly and awkward to get out from under.

He tells me his story during our break. He worked for another collector for about two months until he was caught drunk on the job. Before that, he had years in telephone sales in Las Vegas, selling vacation packages with high volume cold calling. High volume in more ways than one, I want to say, still peeved at being drowned out by his voice.

The trainee who had the run-in with compliance joins in to tell us about his firing from a previous agency. It is a collector's hard-luck story. Beset by car trouble, he had called in late and walked for blocks in the rain. He was soaked through when he arrived, only to be told that he was terminated for tardiness, it being his third offense. What bothers him most is that the firing came two days before the end of the month, beating him out of a bonus payment. Despite his absences, he was able to exceed his goal for the period. But the company kept his bonus and refused to pay him a pro rata share.

The other collectors, or at least the other male collectors, adopt an air of unconcern about getting fired, discussing the fall of others and even their own potential termination with casual bravado. I think there's something about the tough atmosphere of the place that appeals to our machismo. When I talk about the uncertain future that I and my coworkers face, outsiders are perplexed and sometimes a little horrified. One friend of mine wonders how a business could succeed when its workers are not sure they will be there from one month to the next. I explain that there's something energizing about being in a performance-oriented environment. It's like playing a sport— there's no question about what you have and have not accomplished. Everyone can see what you do. Our scoreboard is the dry-erase board at the front of the room, which displays how much money each of us has brought in. The league standings come in a weekly memo from management that lists each collector in the group, in order of his or her collection total. As for play-offs, that would be the monthly bonus assembly, where the top performers in the company receive five-figure bonus checks. We trainees are minor league players who cannot hope to participate in that. Soon, we will watch it as spectators though, and let it nurture our hopes of one day joining the elite.

The agency operates under the principles of a strict meritocracy. If you're not putting money on the board, no amount of office politics is going to do you much good. This is one place where it's not who you know, it's what you know; or rather, what you can do. It's almost impossible for anyone else to claim credit for your accomplishments. And if you do let someone steal an account that you have been working, shame on you. You were caught napping and you lost out—so it is your fault. If you had made the call—that last, successful call—the payment would be yours. The crucial rule is that any payment that comes in within 24 hours of the last call made to an account goes to the collector who made the call, regardless of who takes the payment. This works in tandem with another rule that prohibits more than one call in a 24-hour period, unless it is a follow-up call that the debtor is expecting.

Ironically, the floor is a bullshit-free environment—except for the deceptions routinely practiced on debtors. The tough rules with no exceptions parallel the stance we take with debtors. We don't credit excuses from each other, so why should we listen to theirs? Then again, collecting isn't for everyone. Many of the people who depart don't wait for the ax. One day, for example, Benjamin's seat is empty. He simply stops showing up for work, without a call or a note of explanation. His absence is not remarked on. His friend Aaron tells me that Ben was just "done." The few things he left behind disappear from his desk overnight, and another trainee shortly settles there.

Action Item: Recognize Harassment

Under the FDCPA, collectors may not "harass, oppress or abuse" consumers. Specifically, they may not use obscene or profane language, or call "repeatedly or continuously" to cause annoyance. The law does not say how frequently a collector may call. For more information on this topic, see Chapter 22, "Using Collection Law."

5 ───────────────────────

The Shakedown Industry

Sharing a table in the break room with other trainees, the talk turns to our experiences in the collections world. Arnold, a sharply dressed guy who favors two-tone shirts, tells us what it was like to work at one of the supposed legal firms that dot the suburban office parks around the region. This was a collection office that used the name of a law firm, but Arnold never saw a lawyer in the building. The office focused on collecting bounced checks—"NSF" in collector-speak—obtained by a debt buyer who ran the operation behind the scenes. The collectors worked from a script that made it sound like their "law office" had already drawn up court papers, which they were itching to file. "They'll get the name of the county the debtor is in and say papers are being filed in that county's courthouse in the morning, unless [the debtor] pays now," Arnold told me. To the debt, they added on a "legal fee." "I've seen bills for $200 go up to $900," he said. He claims he was let go for refusing to demand the unjustified and illegal fee. "When they get in trouble, they close one [office] and open up another," he said.

This all sounded very familiar to me. The conversation took place nearly two years after a local lawyer had been disbarred for renting his name to a collection outfit similar to the one where Arnold worked.[1] For payments ranging up to $10,000 per month, attorney John Daniel Lenahan served as the supposed head of the operation. But, in fact, he had little to do with the operation, court cases eventually found. In his resignation from the legal profession, Lenahan admitted that he aided a nonlawyer in the unauthorized practice of law, and that he knew of and "ratified" abusive debt-collection practices. In a court deposition, it came out that others rented the offices, hired the workers, and managed day-to-day operations. The eventual crackdown on Lenahan did not touch the real operators of the business, so they sprang up like a whack-a-mole, forming new companies under new names. The company even filed bankruptcy, stiffing its own creditors—including victims of its collection scams who had won court judgments against the Lenahan firm.[2]

It was this operation that drew my interest to debt collection in the first place. It all started back in 2003 with the shutdown of a tele-sales center in Buffalo. The call center was taking a hit from federal restrictions on telemarketing, which put peoples' home telephones off-limits for telemarketers. At a job fair for the displaced workers, one tipster said that a new company was coming in with plans to reoccupy the building. This new company, he continued, was a law office.

I have heard plenty of incredible news tips, but this one was a doozy. What use could a law office have for a huge call center? The building was a windowless concrete box, originally built as a supermarket, with an asphalt parking lot out front and a loading dock around back. Not exactly the environment for burl walnut desks and leather armchairs. But the tip checked out—if your idea of a law office doesn't require it to have any lawyers present. When the customer service company shut down, the building was taken over by a debt-collection outfit that called itself Lenahan Law Office.

I drove out to take a look, but John Daniel Lenahan was not there when I visited. Instead, I was greeted by a pair of guys in their shirt-sleeves who ran the place. They puffed up with pride as they explained how they had taken over the hive of computer-equipped cubicles. They obviously felt that their business acumen was responsible for recycling the failed call center and filling a hole in the local economy. The state had even pledged them a half-million dollars to retrain the workers, whose previous employer had essentially been put out of business by the federal crackdown against telemarketing.

The more I learned about what went on in the former supermarket, the more intrigued I grew. Before moving there, the collection outfit had operated in a smaller building, using the name of a different lawyer who lived in a town 200 miles away.[3] I tracked down one of the people who had worked in that office. He compared the no-show lawyer with the title character in the movie *Weekend at Bernie's*, in which the deceased owner of a beach house is propped up by his guests in order to keep the party rolling. But the collection law office did not even have the body of a lawyer, just the name of one. People working at the new office told me they were trained for a couple of days before being sent to the collection floor. To bring in money, they would bark demands at people over the phone.

Then, I began to hear from people at the receiving end of the calls. Angry, frustrated, and offended people. Having seen my story about the company's opening, they would call me at the newsroom and splutter about how collectors threatened to seize their home or paycheck and bad-mouthed them to neighbors. Some callers said that collectors had contacted their boss and hinted that they were in trouble with the law. Of all these people, the angriest ones insisted that they didn't owe any money.

When I relayed these complaints to the managers at Lenahan, they bristled with indignation. They said that debtors don't like being told to pay up, so they concoct all sorts of tales to deflect attention from their own actions. These people shouldn't skip out on their bills; that sticks the rest of us with higher prices as a result, as businesses are forced to make up for the delinquent accounts. And these deadbeats certainly shouldn't besmirch the collectors in their effort to weasel out of paying.

But after talking to Lenahan targets from Maine to California, I wasn't buying the self-righteous act. The complaints formed a pattern, as if the threats were delivered from a script. One man who called himself "Officer Pompey" particularly liked to say that police were on their way to take the debtor, or one of his family, off to the county jail. People inside the collection office confirmed the victims' stories. "I heard collectors telling children on the phone, 'the marshals will be there to take your mother and father away,'" one ex-staffer told me. Later, I saw the same threat quoted in court papers that had been filed against Lenahan by the outraged parents of a 14-year-old.[4] Of course people should pay back their legitimate debts. But when they can't, they or their children don't deserve to be terrorized by telephone.

Underlying the Lenahan operation were debts with murky origins, usually old credit card accounts. These accounts came, not from the original lenders, but from dealers in bad debt.[5] The dealers bought and sold "paper," industry slang for unpaid bills. The Lenahan crew bought the supposed debts for a fraction of the unpaid balance, people working at the operation told me. The "paper" was actually a computer spreadsheet of names, addresses, and dollar amounts. Actual paper would have been an improvement. No one at Lenahan had account records proving that the people on the list really owed the money. They took the word of the lender—or rather, the word of the debt dealer who sold the list.

The whole operation seemed absurd: a building full of telesharks, a pile of shaky debts, and a no-show lawyer. But the Lenahan Law Office prospered for years. The state treasury opened to it, and it opened new offices to accommodate its growth. Imitators even sprang up using a similar business model.

The Lenahan crew was onto a hot, moneymaking opportunity. The government had cracked down on telemarketing, the business of calling people and selling them stuff. But the business of calling people and simply demanding money from them was—and is— wide open. Debt collectors face no Do Not Call Registry. In most places, collection agencies do not need a license to operate. They can obtain debts cheaply over the Internet in minutes—if they are not too picky about the accounts' legitimacy. Once they are set up in business, they can obtain consumers' credit reports. This gives them a window into consumers' financial status and helps them track down people at home or at work. They can also sign up for commercial services that supply consumers' phone numbers and addresses.

The Lenahan crew refined this approach to the collection business, but they didn't invent it, I learned. Other outfits across the country had already discovered the profits to be made in cheap, sold-off debts and hardball collection tactics. The evidence that the Lenahan crew wasn't alone can be found in the bulging complaint files of federal and state regulators and consumer watchdog groups.[6]

A prime example was a group of companies known as CAMCO, which the Federal Trade Commission shut down back in 2004 for "threatening and harassing thousands of consumers to get them to pay old, unenforceable debts or debts they did not owe," as the agency put it.[7] The agency's lawsuit laid out the business plan: Obtain old, out-of-date debts and issue false threats to seize property or wages, or even threaten to put people in jail.

"This is a case about a debt collection company gone wild," the FTC's court filing said. "The defendants are in the business of attempting to collect 'time-barred' debts—debts so old that they are beyond the statute of limitations, cannot appear on credit reports, and which are often purchased from other debt collection agencies which have written them off. The defendants have little documentation regarding the original debts, and very often are collecting from people that never owed a debt in the first place. Efforts to collect universally employ a variety of utterly false claims and abusive practices."[8]

What is important to note about CAMCO was that the brazenly illegal conduct did not occur at some small-time operator with a suitcase packed for a quick getaway. This was a Delaware-filed corporation with various operating units, hundreds of employees, and an eight-story headquarters building in Rockville, Illinois—which it owned. "The scale of this fraud is staggering," the FTC said in court papers. "It is collecting millions of dollars each year."[9]

CAMCO's success at raking in cash was not unnoticed by imitators. Despite its scale, and the publicity surrounding the regulatory crackdown, the company's shutdown failed to put a dent in complaints about hardball collection tactics. To the contrary, complaints about third-party collectors have continued to rise steeply, according to the FTC's annual report to Congress. From a total of 34,543 complaints recorded by the agency in 2003, the number jumped nearly 70 percent the next year, the last year that CAMCO was able to operate.[10] The following year, with CAMCO out of business, complaints slowed their rise, but continued on their upward track, growing another 14 percent. By 2008, the most recent year on record, the total had climbed to nearly 79,000, having more than doubled in the span of five years. Among the complaint totals, some of the fast-growing types of complaints involve the sort of practices that CAMCO employed, including demanding debts that consumers don't even owe.

Why wouldn't imitators sprout up? It is not as though CAMCO was unsuccessful. For all the regulatory finger-pointing, no one at the company faced criminal prosecution, so the organizers did not have to worry about jail time. And while CAMCO was fined $1 million, returning some of its ill-gotten gains, the FTC's own court action indicates that the operation was able to bring in several times that much money. The lesson that shakedown artists learned was not to be so visible. Don't buy an eight-story headquarters. In the years since CAMCO's shutdown, the FTC continues to launch one or two high-profile crackdowns on collectors a year, but consumer complaints continue to grow. This indicates that the scammers have learned their lesson, operating from smaller, less visible outfits, split up among multiple offices and locations. In 2008, the FTC heralded its largest-ever penalty against a collector in a crackdown against a Pennsylvania company called Academy Collection Service. The company paid a fine of $2.25 million, and the FTC also went after two supervisors in its Las Vegas office with monetary penalties.[11] But the company admitted no wrongdoing, which might have hurt its ability to obtain accounts, and the original six-figure penalties against the two supervisors were knocked down to $7,500 each.[12] The settlement terms bar the company and the two supervisors from a long list of abusive actions that are already prohibited by federal law, and they are all allowed to continue their work in the industry. Meanwhile, complaints about collection shakedowns continue their upward trajectory.[13]

Upstart collectors aren't the only ones making a buck from rapacious tactics, however. So are some of the nation's biggest lenders, whose sold-off accounts provide fuel for the collection shakedown. Some of the accounts that CAMCO used had originated at mainstream lenders, according to court papers. The Lenahan office also collected on major credit card accounts. Credit card issuers—the same names you see on card offers that drop in your mailbox—are selling off their uncollectable accounts in an open bazaar. The accounts are passed around from hand to hand, to anyone willing to buy. By selling off accounts they couldn't collect themselves, big lenders cash out their charged-off debt—and turn their backs on the tactics used to rake in the money.

Newspaper articles about the lawless law office in Buffalo drew calls and e-mails from browbeaten debtors around the country. I shook my head in sympathy and referred people to the Federal Trade Commission. Imagining the power residing behind the stone pillars in Washington, I thought something would be done. But except for one or two crackdowns a year on the most egregious offenders, the consumer protection agency stands by while consumers clamor for help. Debt-collection law makes consumers responsible for the bulk of enforcement, giving them a "private right of action" with which to take collectors to court.

It is surprising how few collection scammers face criminal prosecution. Using threats to shake people down for money is extortion, after all. One of the rare cases of a criminal court action against a collection agency came about in San Diego County, when a particularly brazen collector collided with a tough prosecutor.[14]

Edward M. Davis set up a company he called ARM Financial. Posing as a lawyer, he and about a half-dozen colleagues at ARM would use the tried-and-true squeeze tactic, telling people that police were on their way to arrest them. The only chance the debtors had of avoiding the imminent trip to jail, Davis said, was to turn over their checking account number immediately, authorizing a withdrawal to extinguish their debt. When the ARM crew called someone with a Hispanic surname, they added threats of deportation to the arrest threat. Ironically, many of the supposed debts had been generated by an investment scam that was shut down years earlier by the state attorney general. Davis "would call people [at work] trying to talk to their bosses—he would get them into a frenzy," Deputy District Attorney Tricia Pummill said in an interview.[15]

This all came out after Davis himself was arrested in San Diego County and pleaded guilty to extortion. Davis' downfall came at the hands of two people. The first was an intended victim whose umbrage spurred him to complain to police and to keep pushing for action. Many of the others targeted by the collection scam, however, were frightened enough by the threats to cough up money. Davis was obliged to return $40,000 to victims of the shakedown scheme.[16] "Most of them told me they don't owe these debts and established to my satisfaction that they don't owe this money," Pummill told me. "Some of them paid it because they were terrified."

The second and critical break for prosecutors came when an employee of ARM breached his silence and admitted that vicious threats, like the deportation threats aimed at Hispanics, were a common practice. Without the employee's inside testimony, the case against Davis would have collapsed, Pummill said, and it would not have been the first time that happened. Collectors faced with debtors' accusations will often deny making threats, clouding the case with doubt. Rarely is there evidence on the debtor's side, like a recording of threats made over the phone, to refute the collector's story. And even when there is evidence of a shakedown, the collector might still evade justice by blaming the actions on a single rogue employee directly involved. This sort of smoke screen is usually thick enough to avert prosecution. It is rare that prosecutors will wade into what looks like a business dispute between two parties, each of whom claims to be the victim. To law enforcement, the scenario looks like the sort of business matter that is for a civil court to hash out. Beneath that smoke screen, scammers like Davis can usually operate with little fear of criminal penalties. "I think there's a lot of this going on," Pummill said in an interview. "I don't think it's rare."

It is one thing to be threatened by a pretend lawyer. Consumers who are aware of these tricks cannot be hurt by them because the scammers have no actual authority to carry out their threats. As Pummill said wryly, police will not come after you for a murky, disputed debt that is many years old—and they will certainly not call to warn you beforehand. But when an actual, licensed attorney becomes involved in collecting "debts" with a murky pedigree, things become much more difficult for the target.

Ask Adam Wisniewski, a manager at a housewares store in upstate New York. He was just about to begin a two-week vacation when his run-in with a legal collection firm began. Thinking he would get some cash and pay his cell phone bill, he inserted his bank card in the ATM machine at the shopping mall. The machine spat the card back out. His account, into which he had just deposited his $800 paycheck, was frozen. When he asked the bank what was going on, they threw up their hands and gave him the name of a law firm that had hung a lock on his money.[17]

A bud of concern began to impinge on his good mood. Adam called the law firm, expecting to straighten out some whacky mix-up and resume his vacation. But the Long Island lawyers weren't kidding around. They had slapped him with a six-year-old court judgment for failing to pay a Citibank Visa card.[18]

Adam was dumbfounded. Not only had he received no word of the court action against him, he never had a Citibank card in the first place. He protested that he was the wrong guy, but this got him nowhere. The law firm offered to unfreeze his account—if he handed over $500 as a down payment and admitted the debt. What he thought was a misunderstanding escalated into a financial nightmare. Instead of enjoying his vacation, Adam sat around the house, dazed at how his earnings had been seized. His calls to Citibank turned up no record that he was ever a cardholder.[19] But neither did the bank have any authority to stop the collection squeeze. The lawyer who froze his account worked for a company that had bought the right to enforce the judgment against him, putting the bank out of the picture. Adam's vacation turned into a trip into debtor's hell, giving him the experience of being flat broke. He had to rely on his girlfriend for basic living expenses for two awkward weeks, until his next paycheck came through.[20]

Having time on his hands, Adam took a trip to the courthouse in Niagara Falls, New York, and studied the case against him. He read the papers that should have been delivered to him years earlier, when the case was filed. What he found surprised him: The collector had been able to seize his money without presenting proof that Adam owed a single dollar. Six years earlier, a company called Platinum Recovery Services went to the courthouse and accused him of skipping out on $2,550 in credit card charges dating back to 1997. The accusation tacked on $510 in attorney's fees. Notably absent from the court file was anything that would back up the claim that he owed the money— not a credit card application with his signature, not a copy of a bill with his name on it, nothing. The accusation didn't even name the credit card that Adam supposedly left unpaid. (He was told it was Citibank when he called the law firm.) Nor did the complaint against him say why Platinum, which isn't a bank, had come looking for the debt. The one-page accusation called the credit card company Platinum's "predecessor in interest," meaning the right to collect the supposed debt had been transferred to Platinum.

Although there were no account records Adam could challenge, there was another intriguing piece of paper in the court file, a statement from a process server who was supposed to have notified Adam about the court date in 2000. The sworn statement said that a court summons was delivered to Adam in person and described him as a blond man in his twenties. The age was right, but Wisniewski's hair is dark brown, almost black. Moreover, he sported a pierced eyebrow at the time, as well as tattoos on his arms. None of these identifying marks was noted in the process server's description.[21]

Unaware of the court date, Adam failed to show up for his own case in a Niagara Falls courtroom in 2001, and a judge brought down the gavel against him. But instead of using the judgment to collect, which it could have done, Platinum inexplicably let the matter sit. The judgment lay dormant like a land mine for years until a different company, represented by another lawyer, used it in the summer of 2006 to freeze his account. The new company, Accounts Retrievable System, had obtained the right to collect the debt from Platinum and hired a Long Island lawyer to put the squeeze on. There was still not a shred of paper on file to show that Adam ever had a Citibank card. But with the power of the court decision behind it, the collector was able to tie up his checking account. It was up to Adam to prove his innocence.[22]

The story didn't surprise Ken Hiller, a Buffalo-area lawyer to whom Adam went for help. Hiller used to help overwhelmed debtors escape their debts by filing bankruptcy, until bankruptcy reform in 2005 made the legal fees prohibitive for many. So he switched to helping people fight aggressive collectors. His new practice is thriving. Bewildered consumers like Adam, with frozen accounts and useless ATM cards, flock to his office.[23]

"I get calls from people every day whose bank accounts are frozen," Hiller told me. "Sometimes the information [collectors] have is a mere address and balance and account number. It's like they shoot first and ask questions later." The system puts the burden on the consumer, who is in the position of proving he didn't have the account, or didn't receive notice of a court date.

Hiller's first move was to challenge the judgment against Adam. He filed a motion to have the judgment struck down. Hiller's appearance on the scene sent the message that Adam wasn't going to just give up. If Hiller kept the pressure up in court, the other side would eventually have to come up with account records or some kind of documentation to show that the supposed debt existed. Adam waited for the origins of his mystery debt to be solved. But, instead of coming up with evidence, the opposing lawyer finally backed down. It dropped the case without an explanation—after tying up Adam's bank account for three months and accusing him of being a deadbeat.[24]

What does the collector have to say? The law firm that froze Wisniewski's account wouldn't discuss the case specifically, but collection lawyers deny that the legal system tilts in favor of collectors. Many cases proceed the way Adam's did because debtors frequently respond to collectors only when their money is seized, they say. Then they often claim to be unaware of the debt and the judgment against them. So cases like Wisniewski's often are not resolved until they reach the stage of court action.

But what about the missing notice to Wisniewski that would have prevented the whole episode, had the court papers reached him? Questionable "process service," or the delivery of court papers, is widespread enough to have earned the nickname of "sewer service" in the legal community. This is a reference to papers that are delivered into a storm drain instead of to their intended recipient. When the defendant fails to show up in court, the resulting default judgment gives the collector the power to seize the defendant's assets. This process nearly succeeded in squeezing the "debt" from Adam Wisniewski. If Hiller had not taken Adam's case on contingency, rather than for an hourly fee, Adam would have had no choice but to give up on his frozen checking account, he told me. Platinum's lawyer wouldn't comment.

In any event, the phantom debt never materialized and Wisniewski got his checking account unstuck, eventually. That makes him one of the lucky ones, according to debtors' attorneys and consumer advocates. Once an account has been seized, many people caught up in a collection action have no choice but to relinquish the money. Hiller believes it happens frequently because it's difficult to hire an attorney in a dispute over a few thousand dollars. Unless the attorney can recover from the opponents on the other side of the dispute, legal fees are likely to consume most of the winnings.

Action Item: Find a Consumer Attorney

To find a lawyer to help you file a lawsuit against a debt collector under the Fair Debt Collection Practices Act, check local antipoverty agencies or the National Consumer Law Center, whose Web address is http://www.consumerlaw.org. For more on this topic, see Chapter 24, "Preparing a Complaint."

6

PIF Means Payment in Full

Once I went to work as a collector, my perspective on debt began to swing around on its axis. I found myself leaning toward the creditor's point of view. Despite having heard consumers' horror stories about unfair and abusive collections, like the seizure of Adam Wisniewski's account, my inclination to take the side of the consumer began to weaken. No wonder, given how rarely I now encountered honest consumers who had truly been wronged. In my daily work as a collector trainee, calling people with debts that had gone unpaid for a year or more, innocent victims of the collection system like Adam were few and far between—and they were mixed in among many people who would simply prefer not to pay.

Over one weekend, I pondered the ways debtors had burned me. They had taken control of the conversation and cast doubt on the debt. They would say that it wasn't really theirs, ask where the proof was, and exclaim how dare someone call them out of the blue with this false and demeaning accusation.

Instead of examining the ways that the office is hornswoggling debtors, I tried to think of ways to answer their denials. The problem is that we didn't have full-blown proof of the debt, such as account slips bearing the debtor's signature. It is doubtful that anyone has kept those. But, eventually, I thought of a way to turn this admission around to my advantage.

Terry Volk was a guy who had apparently skipped out on a $600 credit card balance run up in 2005. Accurint turned up a new phone number for him, in the same state as his original address. The outgoing greeting on his answering machine gave his full name. I heard this greeting several times over the course of a few weeks, as I persistently called and left my message.

Finally, on one of my attempts, he picked up. I presented the standard demand for payment, and he started trying to wriggle free by casting doubt on the legitimacy of the debt. I held firm. The creditor has forwarded us this account information, I told him. It's under your name, and your identifying details match the account record.

"But I think I paid this off a long time ago," he said uncertainly. "In fact, they gave me a refund because I overpaid."

"And a letter discharging the account?"

"No, just the refund."

"That's not the information that I have."

"Well, I won't do anything. I need account records to prove this is mine."

Then I took a breath and tried out my new rebuttal.

"Well, Mr. Volk, if you require nothing less than a full legal standard of proof, that is your right. We can send the account back to the creditor and they will decide whether to go that route," I said. "They will have to dig up the records and show a judge that yes, they have the right guy, and the debt is unpaid. But I'm looking at it right here on your credit report, so there's not really any doubt in my mind how that is going to turn out."

Then I switched gears, lowering the stick and showing him the carrot. "What we do is different from the legal process. In our voluntary process, we take a cooperative approach to resolving the outstanding balance." It is standard practice to refer to our collection action as a "voluntary" or "cooperative" process, implying the possibility of involuntary and uncooperative alternatives. "There are significant benefits to using our process," I continued. "We may even be able to settle this for significantly less than the full balance. But there's really no point in discussing this further unless you commit to working with us to resolve this."

Volk wavered. "Well, I want to know the details," he said. "What kind of deal you are offering?"

I was tempted to tell him about the settlement, but held firm to get his admission of the debt first.

"Sir, unless you are serious about accepting responsibility for this delinquent obligation, it would just be a waste of time to start discussing the payment options. Do you?"

"But..."

"It's a yes-or-no question."

"Well, yes," he mumbled. I could hardly believe it. I had pushed hard and won. I didn't explicitly threaten a lawsuit, which would be illegal. But he had brought up the issue by asking for proof. It is the debtor's right to ask for verification of the debt, but they are to do so in writing, within 30 days of first being contacted. Our first contact with Volk was far more than 30 days before my call, and there was no record of a request for verification of the debt. Therefore, I interpreted his demand for proof as a dispute of the debt, which would result in it being referred back to the client, and as a desire to move the dispute to the legal system, which deals in matters of proof. Because he had brought up the subject, I told him it is the creditor's option to go to court, which is true. My gut check came up clean—we both knew he owed the money and was trying to duck a legitimate debt.

In the end, Volk called back after having talked to his lawyer, or saying he had. He turned down the settlement that was offered and opted to pay the balance in full, an extra $200, because he said it would look better on his credit report.

"That certainly works for us," I said, waving Aaron over to help take the payment. It was only my second one—I almost never use these screens where payments are taken. PIF, I noted on the account status, for payment in full.

Volk was the first of three payers that came in that day for $1,700 in total payments. I used varying degrees of firmness in the "talk-off," but the same pattern. Admit no doubt about the validity of the debt. You want to dispute it, OK. Take your chances. By the end of the day, it will be out of my hands. Whatever settlement I offer will expire at the close of business today. All of that is true, although omitting the fact that a different collector might offer the same terms, or better, on the next call.

The last payer was a woman in Texas whose husband worked in a wood crafting shop. I had called the workplace a couple of times leaving messages. His wife called me back from home. She was mad at the bank, and, fortunately, not at me. When she and her husband got behind on the bills, they asked the bank to close the account and stop the interest, so they could just pay off the balance. But the bank wouldn't do it, she said. It just kept adding the interest and fees until she gave up paying and the account was closed. "It was originally a $200 limit card," she said. The full balance on the account now was over $800. "I'm not paying that; I refuse to pay that." I tried to side with her against the bank, even though we both knew that the bank was indirectly paying my wages. "I'm supposed to say that interest is what happens when charges go unpaid," I said. "But I hear what you're saying. We aren't the bank. We work for them, but we do things differently. Maybe we can work something out." I offered a settlement of 40 percent off the balance, saying I would need to put her on hold for a moment. Then I sat with the phone on mute for 30 seconds while I summarized the call in my notes and listened for whatever she might say to her husband in the interim.

The balance was already five years old, but I didn't tell her it would vanish from her report by itself in two more years, under the U.S. Fair Credit Reporting Act. After all, this isn't consumer protection work. In a business negotiation, it would be foolish to volunteer information that isn't in your interest. When she came back on the line, she was still reluctant to pay. I put her on mute again, supposedly to look into the possibility of a hardship settlement. After twiddling my thumbs another 30 seconds, I came back and asked her if she had faced any "exigent circumstances" that contributed to the delinquency. By instinct, I was starting to sprinkle long, Latinate words into these conversations.

"Were there medical problems? A loss of income? Family issues? We don't have to be specific," I tell her. "Essentially we just have to check a box." Meaning that I need to type something into the blanks in the settlement screen, or else the computer will reject the settlement.

"We've had all of those, but the problem is all the interest,'" she said.

I sighed. "Well, in consideration of your family issues then, we are prepared to offer further reduction of the balance, a 45 percent discount, a savings of almost $400."

That did it. She approved two checks by phone, spread over two months, splitting the settlement. I patted myself on the back for a sharp talk-off. She was probably congratulating herself for bargaining hard and winning an extra discount, on top of the original 40 percent, unaware that I could have given another 5 percent. I had managed to distance myself from the blood-sucking creditor while still invoking its authority. I also kept the highly unlikely possibility of litigation vaguely in the background. Later when I sat in with a real collector on the main collection floor, I'd learn that these tactics are second nature out there, as habitual as breathing.

While my luck was on the rise, others are running out of it. Joe was gone, fired since Friday. There was no fuss about it. I don't know if his dismissal was over compliance, attendance, or just because he's loud and obnoxious. But if he was fired for not abiding by consumer protection law, it made no impression on my coworkers. Bobby is just as loud and vocal with his threatening messages, falsely implying that criminal charges are about to be filed. The other night, one of his monthly payers bounced a check. He called the guy and shouted at him to make up the payment. When a check bounces, the collector has 24 hours to get a makeup payment or else lose the fee—and the account.

"Did you know that bouncing a check across state lines is a federal offense?" he barked into his phone. I almost laughed at the image of a giant check bouncing across the state border. The image in the debtor's mind probably wasn't as humorous.

"Will that clear?" Bobby said later during the call, in a lower voice, having extracted a promise to pay. "How much money is in your account?" Having the starch to demand information like that, without hesitation, is what makes him the most successful collector in the training group. That, and his willingness to sling false threats.

While Bobby was painting a picture of handcuffs and federal marshals for his debtor, I was hearing the hardest of hard-luck stories. The husband said the debtor was sleeping; she was sick. I said it was very important and he should wake her up. The 60-ish woman in rural Mississippi mumbled sleepily that she didn't have the money, not even $110 for a minimum down payment on the $1,100 balance. She said she'd be able to pay something in two weeks. I asked, what happens in two weeks? She mumbled something indistinct. Like most debtors, she had been sick, supposedly, but none of the telltale traces of medical bills appeared on her credit report. Apparently, she'd paid them off without trouble, or she had good insurance. She was also having no trouble making payments on a $12,000 car loan. She was also up to date on her $319 mortgage payment. The $39,000 mortgage looked to be about one-quarter paid off already. But being paid up on some bills does not earn you any slack from a collector. Just the opposite.

"You have a nice car, you have equity in your home—you have the resources to pay this bill, but you're just refusing to use them," I said, using the standard rebuttal from my training manual.

"I'm not refusing," she said, sounding near tears. "I just don't have it." Whether she was distraught from my demands or just tired and sick, she sounded genuinely distressed. But I did not let her off the phone. She said her son helped her buy the car; it wasn't really hers. Well, why shouldn't he help her pay this overdue bill, if he bought her a nice car? And as far as her having no income—debtors almost always say that unless I reach them at their workplace. I took another page from the manual and suggested she take out a home equity loan. The interest will probably be less than the rate she would have to pay on the charged-off credit card debt, I argued, without knowing whether this would turn out to be true. But she hadn't heard of such a thing as a home equity loan. Finally, she hung up saying that I should call back tomorrow. Ah, tomorrow, the day that never comes in this business. As I hung up, I thought of the sign you still see hanging in some bars that says "free beer tomorrow."

"You're cleaning up," Aaron says to me as we file out for break. Tacked at the front of the room, by the board that shows our daily performance, is a list of our names and some columns of numbers beside them. The figures display how much fee we've collected so far, number of days worked, and a calculation extending that rate of performance out to the end of the training period. Rates greater than our goal of $2,500 are highlighted. My rate is a little over $3,000, shaded in gold marker. It hardly seems possible that I am first in my training class. It is rare that I talk to a debtor, much less collect something. But the three hits on my big Monday have lifted me to the top. I walk back to my desk in a daze, feeling a mix of pride and confusion. Now when I come back from the front of the room, just returning from a break, eyes turn toward me down the row of cubes, to see if I'm writing another score on the board. The recognition feels good. If I continue to work here long enough, I will probably learn how to convince an elderly woman to refinance her home in order to pay off an old credit card bill. A month ago, working as a reporter, I would have been disgusted that someone advised that woman in Mississippi to put her home at risk in order to pay off the interest and fees that had built up on a credit card balance.

Maybe my karma is being helped by my off-hours activities. I hear back from an acquaintance who was being hounded by collectors for a hospital bill after missing a single payment. I had advised her to call the hospital's billing department and ask them to pull the account back from the collector. She had a long-term payment arrangement worked out with the hospital, but she missed a single payment through simple inattention. That probably triggered the automatic transfer of her account to the collector. Of course, the collector demanded that she pay the balance in full, immediately, ignoring the previous monthly payment arrangement. Why? Because she could afford to pay it. She had a steady income and good credit. As she recounted their rough insistence, I recognized the tactics straight out of my own employer's playbook. Demand PIF. Look at the debtor's ability to pay. Get the money. It's exactly what I would do, or try to do, if her account had popped up on my screen. The collector must have felt a rush when he saw the account. Here was a fresh bill, untouched by other collectors, with a good working phone number and strong ability to pay. It's the sort of profile that gets a collector's heart beating faster.

"The hospital took back the account," my acquaintance said. "I told them how mean the collectors were." Now she was back on the monthly payment plan.

"That's good," I said to her. "You don't want to deal with those collectors if you can help it." I thought of my counterparts somewhere who had been deprived of a fee. They must be groaning and gnashing their teeth at the loss of this fat account. In their circumstances, that is just how I would feel.

Action Item: Seek Help from the Creditor

Some creditors, but not all, will pull your account from a collection agency if you ask them to do so. It might be possible to start or resume a periodic payment arrangement to settle the bill, and the creditor might offer better terms than the collection agency. For a discussion of settling debts, see Chapter 25, "Negotiating a Debt Settlement."

7

Payday, the Tables Turn

Friday is payday—my first. Checks are distributed at noon, just as we stream out of the building for lunch.

"There's $5 for anybody who will drive me to the bank," loud Gary broadcasts to the corners of the room. I take him, saying I am going anyway. Bobby gives us directions to the bank that handles our company's payroll account, thinking our checks will be easier to cash there. On the way over, Gary tells me how he got canned from his last collecting job, even though his family had connections with the company. The problem was a "liquid lunch" he just couldn't resist one Friday. "Seven martinis," he says, chortling. "I came back to the office. They sent me right from there to rehab."

A relative of his, a debt buyer with business ties in the collection industry, had lined up the job. This was after he hit bottom with drugs and gambling in Las Vegas. It started with back problems that got him on Vicodin, and he slid from there into habitual painkiller use, along with the booze. "I had to run for my life," he said. It is hard to imagine this beefy barrel of a guy in the lifestyle of a high roller in Vegas. He lives in a halfway house from which he is being evicted for some infraction; he says he was caught taking care of a stray cat in violation of the no-pets policy. The place is on my route to work, so I ask him about car pooling to split the gas. He agrees to start at the beginning of next month, when his bus pass runs out.

The bank charges us $7.50 each to cash our paychecks. It is a bigger hit for Gary than for me, with my full two-weeks' pay. "I'm only making $9.50 an hour," he admits as we rush back, gunning through yellow lights and cruising a drive-through for a warm bag of fast food. "I'm making less than anybody here." Whether that's true or not, there are certainly people with no industry experience making more, including me. He had worked at the previous agency for three months. Before that, he'd done years of telemarketing. In Vegas, the vacation packages he hawked on the phone earned him a commission of $270 for each sale. "Some days, I'd sell two, some days only one." Money right in his pocket, usually over $1,000 a week. I wonder about the sort of vacation packages that reaped enough profit to pay a $270 sales commission. The work is similar to collecting, he says—lots of calls, lots of hang-ups and chewing outs, and very few hits. "It's a numbers game."

He insists that I take $2 for gas, even though I steered him into possibly the highest check-cashing fee in the state. Bum steer, I tell them back at the office, recounting the exorbitant fee.

"Isn't that illegal?" one coworker asks. "It should be." We reflect on the irony of getting gouged by a bank for cashing our paychecks, the same paychecks that we earn by enforcing the bank industry's gouging practices on others. We collectors have our own financial problems, yet instead of easing them, payday seems to bring them to the fore. After lunch, Bobby is arguing on the phone with a creditor of his own. "I'll give you my whole check next week," he says, which makes no sense because we are paid biweekly. "If I give you this I'll be walking around with nothing in my pockets." It could have been a parent with him on the phone, or a loan shark.

"I messed up my credit," he explains to us when he's off the phone. He used to park his car in the lot next door to evade the repo guy's tow truck, until the neighboring company finally slapped a bright yellow boot on his front wheel, providing a fascinating spectacle for the collectors on our side of the building. A memo went around the office sternly warning against parking in the lot next door, but the agency helped Bobby smooth things over with the neighbor and retrieve his car. Bobby just laughed off jibes about his faulty sense of direction. The entire episode failed to put a damper on his buoyant charm.

My own financial habits lean toward the other extreme. While people like Bobby enjoy the additional consumption they can afford by borrowing, my instinct is to avoid debt. Maybe this predisposes me to see the creditor's side of things. Yet debtors' stories often show that it wasn't their choice that forced them to borrow, but necessity. Illness, job loss, even car trouble can throw people's budgets off the rails.

Like debt itself, debt collecting isn't always entered into willingly. One evening, Mabel, the group manager and an experienced collection pro, tells a few of us the story of how she wound up in the business by default. She had started out working in customer service for a telephone company in the South. After her job was cut in a downsizing, she moved north to this area of New York State to take care of her aging mother. And where were the entry-level jobs? Collection agencies.

She's been in collections "forever" she said, shaking her head. She dreams of moving back to the South when her mom doesn't need her, back to a warm climate where a two-foot snowfall is unthinkable. But there are few collection operations there where she could readily pick up her career. Whatever the job's drawbacks, collection work has provided for her and her family, which includes a son who is attending a private college. We try to name all the collection offices we know of within commuting distance, but we lose count before we run out of names.

There are copies of a new status sheet posted at the front of the room with everyone's name and collection total listed. I don't have any postdated checks pending, but I've collected about $500 in fee so far this month, more than any of the trainees in my class except two. "Money today" seems to be my motto as well as the company's. None of that long-term payout stuff for me. Gabe sticks out his hand for me to shake and tells me I'm doing well. I smile back at him. I feel proud.

On the drive home, I see that the agency down the street has a sign out by the roadside offering jobs at $16 an hour, part-time, nights, and weekends. This is a new agency, whose owner told me in an interview that they record every collection call in full, to ensure compliance with consumer protection law. Maybe they have to pay the relatively high wage because, if they're seriously following all the rules on every call, no one can make any bonus money.

Action Item: Recognize False Threats

Collection agencies cannot seize your property or garnish your wages without a court judgment. They cannot legally tell other people, such as employers or relatives, about your debts without your permission. Nor can they initiate a criminal complaint against you for fraud. For more about the rules that govern collectors, see Chapter 22, "Using Collection Law."

8

Debtors' Rebellion

Although we aren't warm toward debtors, neither do we collectors have any feelings of fellowship toward the lenders who make our livelihood possible. We know that the banks are hardly blameless in the battle between creditors and debtors. In fact, Congress outlawed many common credit card practices in the Credit Card Accountability, Responsibility, and Disclosure (Credit CARD) Act, which was enacted in May of 2009. The act restricted overlimit fees, limited surprise interest rate hikes, and banned the practice of raising rates retroactively on a balance that is in good standing. In attendance at the bill-signing ceremony was credit card user Janet Hard, a nurse and mother from Michigan. She had seen her interest rate jump to 24 percent retroactively, not only on new purchases, but also on her existing balance—even though she was paying her bill on time. As a result, she made payments totaling $2,400 in one year, but saw her overall debt decline by only $350.

The response of credit card issuers to the CARD Act was predictable. Several used the time lag before implementation to ratchet up their fees and interest rates, in advance of the effective date in early 2010. "Congress in good faith provided credit card companies [nine months] to implement these consumer reforms. But these companies responded by raising interest rates, imposing excessive fees, and tightening credit on consumers before the reforms could even take effect," U.S. House Speaker Nancy Pelosi said in a statement announcing an effort to speed up the implementation of CARD Act protections.[1]

For all the politicians' chest-thumping over their long-awaited crackdown on credit card abuses, there are two important points to consider about the reform: It did not cap rates that card issuers can charge, and it does not apply retroactively to debt that was rung up previously. Unpaid balances that were boosted by outlawed practices like retroactive rate increases and multiple overlimit fees do not get rolled back. The billions of dollars in credit card outstanding debts do not go down by a penny. It is this balance, or the delinquent portion of it, that collectors are working to bring in, and will continue to chip away at for years to come.

If you want to dispute this state of affairs, many card issuers will steer you into a system of mandatory arbitration, a kangaroo court that they control, with predictable results. A study by Public Citizen showed that arbitrators, paid handsomely by the credit card issuers, deliver decisions in favor of the card company 96 percent of the time. Unlike court, there is no recourse for an unfair award.[2] The arbitration system is so blatantly one-sided that one of the main arbitration companies has been driven out of the business by the cost of legal cases against it—including charges of fraud brought by the state of Minnesota. Some major card issuers have dropped the requirement that customers submit to arbitration and give up their rights to be heard in court. Yet the banking industry as recently as mid-2009 still defended arbitration as a practice that can lower the cost of dispute resolution.[3]

Many people in debt bondage to their credit card payments, however, aren't willing to accept the status quo any longer. From my frontline position, I see a debtors' rebellion brewing. Two debtors of the four or five I reach during a single afternoon angrily refuse to pay their balance. Like the woodworker in Texas, they're mad at the bank. They don't deny that the account is theirs, and that it remains unpaid. Their argument is that the supposed debt is not legitimate in the first place. The balance is laden with fees and high-rate penalty interest, they say. Hardly any of the amount due is money they actually borrowed and spent. A construction worker I reach on his cell phone says his supposed $1,200 balance came about on a card that had a $200 limit. He said he'll be glad to pay the $200, but only $200—an amount that is far less than the settlement amount that the creditor is offering.

We lack the detailed financial records necessary to see whether he's exaggerating the fees, but his credit report supports his story. His was a limited-balance card, the kind that banks used to issue willy-nilly to high-risk borrowers. After his balance hit $200 and became delinquent, his ability to make charges was shut off; however, the interest and penalties kept on coming.

Other debtors have similar stories. In response, I parrot the stock speech that Brad taught us: Interest is what happens when you make charges and don't pay them. The creditor's stance is that the terms were laid out in the contract. The cardholder's own actions brought about the debt that they now want to renounce. These costs are all avoidable—just don't pay late, don't go over the limit, or don't make charges in the first place. If you didn't like the deal, why did you sign up for the card?

"The contract that you signed when you opened the account obligates you to pay these charges," collectors say. Referring back to the contract reminds the debtor of the legal arena, where the dispute could potentially end up. It also invokes the image of a two-sided deal, in which the cardholder is now failing to keep up his end of the bargain. But what a bad bargain it is for the consumer.

With late fees, overlimit fees, and penalty interest rates, a supposedly low-balance card can quickly turn into a financial black hole. Near the end of our shift one day, Julie explains to a group of us at the end of the row why the settlements that we can offer are so steep, up to 50 percent off the balance. Many of these were low-limit cards, the kind that are easiest to get, even for high-risk applicants. The ceiling for charges was supposed to be as low as $200 or $300. Then we see the balance has ratcheted up to $1,000 or more. "They're making so much interest on these," Julie says, "that's why they can afford to settle at 50 percent—they're still making a huge profit."

Although our meat is the credit card account, some mornings we arrive to find an entirely different sort of account waiting for us to work. Things like bounced checks and overdraft fees are pretty straightforward. Then there are some debts that we didn't even know existed.

"This stuff is crap," someone in a neighboring carrel says as we get a first look at the accounts we were supposed to work that day. I nod my head in silent agreement. Gabe had called out the name of the WIP (work in progress) and we had obediently begun working the accounts. These turned out to be years-old debts with bad phone numbers, some with no phone numbers, and some not even over the $500 threshold for ordering a credit report.

"What do I do with this?" I ask the screen. The cursor blinks. There is the name of the debtor, and that's it—no phone number, no address, not even the state. Unless I somehow happen to know the debtor personally, I'm out of luck.

The creditor is another mystery, something called an acceptance company whose name we'd never heard before. It isn't a bank or a credit card issuer, but some obscure finance operation.

"It's retail financing," Gabe explains offhandedly. Single-purpose loans for goods sold on an infomercial.

Bobby's on the phone, having a hard time explaining just what the bill is for. The original creditor on our records, the acceptance company, did not ring a bell with the debtor. Bobby cups his hand over the mouthpiece and asks what the merchandise was that these people had bought.

Gabe deadpans it. "Bed-wetting equipment."

The entire pod goes silent a moment while this sinks in. Then we crack up. "Seriously?" Gary asks.

"Yeah, bed-wetting equipment," Gabe says, managing to keep a straight face. "You buy this—thing, whatever—to stop pissing the bed, or for your kids." He doesn't know how the device is supposed to work. Maybe it sets off an alarm when it senses a nocturnal loss of control. Maybe it zaps you with an electric shock when its circuitry determines that an accident is in the making. We don't want to have to ask the debtors to find out.

"Bed-wetting," Bobby shouts to his elderly debtor on the phone. "BED-WETTING! You bought this to stop wetting the bed!" Silence. Then in a lower voice he continues, "Oh…your son bought it? Well, is your son there?" As we work the accounts, it becomes clear that the debtors are not very apologetic about stiffing this company on their bills. Their complaints form a pattern: The thing didn't work—at least not for them. Even if they manage to pack it up and ship it back within the guarantee period, they are hit with fees and shipping costs, on top of a punishing interest rate. The device is a scam, so the finance charges are a scam on top of a scam. They're not paying, and some of them act as though they would love to be taken to court, where they could tell a judge about the rip-off they have suffered. These debtors sense that the creditor probably doesn't want to get anywhere near a courthouse.

I start cutting a swath through my portion of the accounts, secretly hoping that nobody answers my calls. I don't want to try pressuring one of these deeply disgruntled consumers. I don't want to have to talk with strangers about the idiosyncrasies of their urinary tract. Beyond that, I feel sorry for these people. The object they had pinned their hopes on has become another problem that only adds to their suffering. It wasn't casual overspending that got them into this debt—but desperation.

Aaron down the row is getting grilled. He's having to explain why he is privy to information that is both medical and intensely personal. My coworker hems and haws. The debtor apparently believes there's an expectation of privacy for medical purchases. That might be true in your doctor's office or at the pharmacy, but not when you order from an infomercial and hand over your billing information to some finance company. Besides, this device seems beyond the periphery of the medical establishment.

Later, a friend of mine wonders, after I tell her the story, how we came to be working such lousy accounts. The paper was apparently bought by some intermediary, a debt buyer, and farmed out to us. That's probably why it was given to us trainees to work, so as not to waste the time of experienced collectors.

The basic process of the collection industry should let weak debts like this fall to the bottom of the pile, as a natural result of the profit motive. Paper with shaky legitimacy, the offshoot of a borderline consumer scam in the first place, will be hardest to collect, and contingency collectors won't waste much time on it. That, in turn, would result in giving a measure of protection to consumers. At least, that's how it should work. But now that hardball collectors are proliferating, their arm-twisting threats can squeeze money even from the wobbliest debts. Once my agency gives up on these accounts, they might continue sifting down the collection food chain, winding up with some bottom-feeder. As a result, these people hoodwinked into ordering the device might face a barrage of harassment and ruthless threats to pay for it, plus all the finance charges. I can imagine what a CAMCO or a Lenahan-type outfit would do with these accounts. They'd threaten court and use the debtor's embarrassment against them, saying that their purchase of a bed-wetting prevention device would be publicly revealed—the almost literal airing of dirty laundry.

That's the tactic used on Edmund Vandegenachte, whose tussle with a collector I wrote about in a newspaper story. The Ohio-based collector specialized in dunning for a particular kind of bill: phone-sex charges. To the usual threats of arrest and jail, the collector added the threat of public humiliation. Edmund's neighbors, his wife, and even his kids would find out just how he had run up the unpaid bill, the collectors threatened, once this matter went before the court.

Instead of caving in under the pressure, though, the beleaguered house painter consulted a legal clinic, which helped him file a successful lawsuit against the Ohio company.[4]

Later, we are taken off the difficult accounts and mercifully return to working old bounced checks and credit card delinquencies. I find myself skip-tracing accounts worth only a couple of hundred dollars. This is against company policy. The potential payoff doesn't justify the investment of time. But my instinct is to go after people who have ditched their old address and phone number. I wanted to find them and demand payment. The rules call for working easier accounts first—always go for the quick hit, the training binder says. Thus, the sinners are let off the hook, while the righteous are called to account.

Even tracking down a skip is no guarantee of payment, however. "Is Bill there?" I said on one call, having traced a debtor named William to his new workplace, a tattoo parlor in Florida. Bill came on the line and I told him the balance.

"I don't have it," he said.

"That may be," I said, "but taking it from a bank isn't a solution."

"Do what you hafta," he replied. "Go ahead, put a judgment on, it wouldn't be the first. I don't worry about stuff like that." He described himself as a gypsy, an itinerant artist whose canvas was human skin. Maybe he could pay something in the spring, when things picked up. His business was seasonal, tied to cycles of beach vacations and binge drinking. He wouldn't update his address. "I don't worry about mail man. I don't like bills."

"No one likes them," I said. "But something like a bounced check could become a serious problem if you don't step up and resolve it."

"Oh no man, it's not like a criminal thing is it?" Bill said, concern for the first time entering his tone. "I don't want to mess with anything like that."

This looked like my chance to reel him in. All I had to do was play up the image of handcuffs and prison bars, which he had already supplied. Then again, he had offered this scenario readily, perhaps hoping to draw me into an illegal threat.

"I honestly don't know what the creditor will do next," I said instead, hoping the ambiguity would play on his imagination. But Bill wasn't one to worry about the future.

"Well, man I travel a lot—I'm going to Switzerland soon," he said. "Stay cool."

Too many of these rebuffs can get a collector down. Underneath his robust good humor, my pod-mate Gary was growing discouraged. During an evening shift, I overheard him talking to several debtors, so I envied him. I couldn't even get people on the phone. But he wasn't able to bring them around.

"Buncha people swore at me today," he sighed at quitting time. There was a sudden heavy snowstorm and he asked for a ride home. Avoiding the snowy on-ramp to the expressway, I drove all the way into the city on local streets, a stoplight at a time. "Can you stop in real quick at that liquor store?" he said. I pulled into the unplowed lot.

"I hope this doesn't blow your 30 days in detox," I said.

He laughed heartily, which I took to mean that his period of abstinence was already history. He came back with a $10 bottle of orange-flavored vodka. The next morning, he admitted that he downed half the bottle after I dropped him off. He asked if I could smell it on him, and said he wasn't even very hung over, just "a little around the edges." The supposedly alcohol-free house is about to evict him anyway; plus, the pipes there are frozen. "I haven't had a shower since Sunday," Gary said. I flinched back from him about a foot, triggering his big laugh.

As the week wore on, we could hear Bobby using his "fraud investigator" ruse more often. At one point, Aaron was trying to pick it up, but his voice sounded halfhearted, and he dropped it. The trick prompts the debtor to call back, thinking they are being alerted to fraudulent use of their credit card. Then when they call, the fraud accusation is turned against them. During the talk-off, Bobby implies that the debtor defrauded the credit card issuer simply by running up the bill and then failing to pay. "Are you trying to commit fraud?" he will ask. I'm with Aaron: As hardened as I have become, it is hard to imagine pulling off something like that—at least not yet.

At one point, we work a grab bag of charged-off credit cards and store credit accounts. They come not from the credit issuers but from an intermediary, a debt buyer. The old account records are often incomplete, missing a date or correct address. Sometimes, even the debtor's name is mangled with typos. The few people I reach protest that the bill was paid off previously, or that they know nothing about it. One guy started laughing when I shot off my spiel about his balance being seriously delinquent.

"One of you people just called me a few minutes ago," he said.

I checked the account notes, but it wasn't us. No call had been logged for several days. It could be that he was trying to weasel out, but his response was unhesitating and his tone genuinely aggrieved. "You mean someone else is calling me on this?" he said. "I've got two collectors coming after me for the same thing?"

I kept to my guns and told him that we were the ones he had to deal with, not knowing if his tale of two collectors was true. But internally, I checked some mental notes. This complaint sounded familiar to one I had heard before, in a different context.

Action Item: Obtain Your Credit Reports

Knowing what is on your credit report is a key to dealing with debt and debt collectors. Under the U.S. Fair Credit Reporting Act, you are entitled to a free copy of your credit report from each of the three major reporting bureaus: TransUnion, Experian, and Equifax. Avoid paid services claiming "free" access and obtain the reports through the Federal Trade Commission's approved Web site, www.annualcreditreport.com.

9

Debt for Sale

When Harold Wood returned to Long Island after a three-year stint of work in Indonesia, he had some unfinished business waiting for him. A costly divorce and a jobless stretch in his past had left his finances in shambles. So when multiple bill collectors found him and began calling, he wasn't surprised. He acknowledged the debts and agreed to make regular payments via electronic withdrawals from his checking account. "There was one investigator...telling me to go home and kiss my wife and kids goodbye because I would be in court the next day," Wood said. "It made life really interesting. When the third collector called, I hit the total panic button."

The multiplying payments were eating into the money he needed for rent and utilities. At the urging of a credit counselor, he dug up his old bills to find out the depth of his financial hole. The result shocked him. He discovered that three different collectors were dunning him for the same charges he had run up years before on a platinum Visa card. They hadn't divided the debt between them; each collection agency was grabbing for the entire $14,000 that Wood had borrowed. (Late fees ran up the debt to a larger sum, which he disputed.) He had not realized this immediately because he dimly remembered using more than one credit card in the past. More important, the collectors did not refer to the original number on his old credit card, which would have quickly revealed the triple billing. Instead, each collector issued him a different account number, which they had created for their own internal records. But underneath the welter of seemingly unrelated claims was the same debt. In effect, his unpaid balance had somehow multiplied by three. And the worst part was, the collectors had access to his checking account.

Wood stopped feeling like a penitent debtor when he realized he was being scammed. He sent letters to the three collectors demanding they stop sucking money out of his account. Until one of them showed him some proof that they were the legitimate holder of his obligation, all three could wait for payment. Wood said he felt like he was living a nightmare. He was paying and paying, but his debt wasn't going down. Instead, it had multiplied. After he sent the letter, one of the collectors took $1,000 from his checking account anyway, he said in court papers.[1] It was at that point that he went to see a consumer lawyer to try to end the collection nightmare.

What the lawyer found out provided a window into the world of debt buying. Wood's unpaid account had been sold on the debt market by the original credit card issuer, First USA. Then, the account was resold by others until it somehow got into the hands of multiple collectors, Wood's court complaint charged.[2] All three claimed to be the legitimate holder of the debt. One collection lawyer whose office was dunning Wood told me that this was not the first dispute of its kind. It had happened before. Debt sellers had passed him accounts to collect that turned out to have more than one owner. But the collection lawyer denied wrongdoing, saying that he relied on his clients, the debt buyers, to have clear title to the account that was shipped to him for collection.

Buying and selling people's overdue debts might sound odd, but it's a hot idea in some financial circles. Investors buy $100 billion a year in old credit card bills alone—plus more in telephone bills, auto loans, doctor bills and other obligations, according to an analysis by industry research firm Kaulkin Ginsberg in Bethesda, Maryland.[3] The size of the debt-purchase market indicates that it has grown to rival the traditional fee-based collection business, in which lenders retain ownership of their accounts and farm them out to collection agencies.

Virtually all major credit card companies sell portfolios. Debt brokers have sold accounts from Chase, HSBC, Fleet, Bank of America, and other major card issuers. Buyers can bid over the Internet and download account information in minutes. The accounts often include Social Security numbers, along with addresses and phone numbers, to confirm debtors' identities. The buyers of the overdue bills hire collectors to bring in the money, or collect it themselves through their own collection arm. Agencies increasingly form debt-buying units to boost their profits and shield themselves from the ups and downs of the fee-based business, where the loss of a big client can mean a sudden drop in revenue. Most accounts sold on the debt market cost less than 5 percent of the balance due, so the potential profit is high. Buyers of these debts expect to triple their money in five years.

According to the debt-purchase industry, consumers benefit from all this by getting a chance to settle debts for less than their bank would accept.[4] Because the accounts sell at a steep discount, debt buyers can write off much of the original loan and still make a profit.

But some debt buyers aren't so tenderhearted, as the FTC's experience with CAMCO in 2004 showed. The records of the FTC's shutdown showed that the Illinois company bought years-old credit card accounts that originally came from mainstream lenders, fueling the shakedown scam.[5] Some retailers have sold debts for decades, but major lenders didn't join in until the 1980s, when the S&L bailout created a market for unpaid loans.[6] After the bailout ended, investors started scooping up loans from healthy banks. Banks might screen their initial buyers, but few restrict the resale of debts, allowing the accounts to circulate indefinitely. Contracts for debt sales can require the buyers to resell only to reputable companies. But once the sale of the debt is complete and the accounts have been turned over to their new owner, the creditor has little control over what happens next.

Debt brokers say that problems like the one Harold Wood encountered are minor. Sellers would quickly get wind of an unscrupulous operator selling debts multiple times and shut them out of the market, brokers maintain. But financial regulators are not so sure. One Federal Trade Commission official and a state regulator in New York both said in interviews that the practice of debt buying might be at the root of the wave of complaints they are seeing. Once the debt is sold, whatever oversight a creditor might do to protect its reputation is no longer present.[7]

But as a collector, your job is to work with the account records put in front of you. The assumption is that they are genuine, until proven otherwise. Debtors might be lying about the legitimacy of the debt— it's their first tactic to stall and wriggle out of paying. After all, "lying rides upon debt's back," Benjamin Franklin wrote in *Poor Richard's Almanac*. The perspective that works for a collector is to believe strongly that whoever picked up the phone is the debtor, and proceed accordingly. Wrong person? We've heard that before. Already paid? Stop playing games. Keep the pressure on them and who knows, if it really is the debtor, it might work; call their bluff. And if not, well, the worst you have done is to anger someone in a far-off city. You haven't done anything illegal, just rude. But that's business—this business, anyhow. You need to unlearn habits of politeness and civility that condition people to avoid confrontation. Stop allowing others to save face. Stop believing what anyone tells you. Distrust is the rule. Only demonstrations of good faith count for anything, and that means one thing: money—money today. That happens to be the informal company motto, repeated each morning by one of our managers in the huddle as our guiding principle.

Action Item: Dispute Errors on Your Credit Report

You can dispute inaccurate or incomplete information on your credit report under the Fair Credit Reporting Act. For example, information about most types of debt should no longer appear on the report after seven years. To begin the dispute process, send a letter to the reporting bureau with a copy to the originator of the disputed information, usually the creditor. Set out the reason for your dispute and include copies of supporting documentation. For more on credit reports, see Chapter 21, "Checking Out a Collector."

10

The Golden Rule: Money Today

It's a simple maxim—money today—but the people who live by it are well rewarded. This lesson is impressed on my fellow trainees and me during bonus assembly, a monthly event where bonus checks are handed out to the most successful collectors. We are herded out of our training area to an open space by the elevators where we can see the collection floor. In the room's main aisle, a manager with a cordless microphone and a voice like a game-show host hands out the top 20 checks in reverse order, working his way up to the month's biggest hitter. The highest total was $12,600. A woman in an untucked flannel shirt and blue jeans walked up to get her handshake and envelope, to our applause. A disproportionate share of the top bonuses went to women, who are a minority on the floor. "She did that last month too," dapper Arnold standing next to me said. We trainees are huddled against the back wall to watch. None of us are in line for a check of any size. Only floor collectors are eligible, and only after they meet their monthly goal, which ranges from $4,000 to $6,000, depending on the department. Amounts above the goal determine your bonus.

"Every month, she's one of the top," Arnold continues. I comment that a $12,000 monthly bonus, on top of regular pay and benefits, would make for a comfortable living. I calculated how long it would take to stockpile a fund that would allow me to take a year off and bike around Europe. Then I wondered how many of my fellow trainees were performing similar calculations of their own. Just one month like that would wipe out their debts, or bring their child-support payments current and get their ex-wife off their back, maybe even win them a little respect. Another few months would put them in a Hummer or Lincoln Navigator. A few months beyond that, they would be standing at the doorstep of a suburban mini-mansion, down payment in hand. These are guys who've never earned much more than minimum wage, and many of them don't have a checking account. At the bonus assembly, their dreams parade before them, close enough to reach out and touch.

On an evening shift, shortly after bonus assembly, I train with one of the highest performers on the floor—one of those people in line for the big bonus checks. Barbara is a dark-haired woman with no makeup and unstylish, country-style blue jeans. But when she speaks, she sounds like an actress. The company supplies her with a plush, executive-type office chair and a new flat-screen PC on her desktop, not the older PCs that most floor collectors use—and certainly not one of the antique terminals that trainees struggle with. Her booth is plastered with pictures of a grinning blonde girl who looks about four or five years old. I plug my phone cord into the extra jack on her phone to hear both sides of her conversations with debtors.

She hits auto-dial and whips through screens at a blur, taking in a debtor's account record and credit report in a glance. She builds a picture of their finances while listening to their phone ring. By the time someone picks up, she has found the amount of their mortgage, and used that to make an educated guess about their income and the equity built up in their home. She has found out where they like to shop, and how much they spend in a typical month using their charge cards. She even checks the other entities that have ordered the debtor's credit report. If a tax return service has obtained the report, for example, she knows that a tax refund loan might be in the works. On the other hand, if several other collection agencies have already obtained the report, the signs are unpromising. The debtor in this scenario has probably "blown up," or gone delinquent on all their obligations at once, and is flooded with dunning calls.

One account that Barbara pulls up is for a charge account that had been run up to its maximum and then closed out as delinquent, all in less than a year.

"Oh, oh," I say, "looks like fraud."

"Maybe, but fraud is usually family fraud," Barb says. She is eager to work the account. "I get paid on family fraud."

Collectors are aware that much identity theft is a family affair. The magical piece of plastic lying on the dresser becomes a temptation too difficult to resist, and a son or daughter filches the card and rings up charges on it, forging the parent's signature. Less often, a family member opens a new card in the name of a relative or a housemate without their knowledge.

In either case, our response is the same. The cardholder is told they can either pay the bill, or file a police report against the offending family member who ran up the charges. I have heard the talk-off before—it is the tactic that Gabe told Benjamin to use on one of his debtors. If the cardholder is claiming to be a victim of identity theft, he or she should take the obvious next step and report the crime. We offer to hold off on further dunning calls if they fax us a copy of their police report.

Barbara was able to determine that a male family member lived at the same address as our debtor. At first, he looked like a spouse, having the same last name as the debtor, but his birth date put him 20 years younger. "It's probably the son," Barbara said. "The woman might not even know about these charges."

On that evening though, no one answered the phone and I didn't get to hear Barbara put the arm on them. When she reached an answering machine, she left a message that sounded like she was reading from a legal script. "This call will be recorded for compliance purposes," she began in a bored tone. Indeed, our compliance department just might be listening in on the call to monitor Barb's adherence to debtor protection law. But her message implied that the tape was for an altogether different purpose. Her phrasing indicated that the recording was meant to document that "our firm" had given the debtor every opportunity to respond to the "pending matter." She sounded just like a disinterested paralegal issuing a mandatory disclosure, completing one last rote chore before a lawsuit could be filed. She even made the mini-Miranda warning sound ominous by emphasizing that she was "required by law" to disclose that the call was an attempt to collect a debt.

"As you can tell, my message isn't legal," she said to me quietly after terminating one of these calls. "Compliance hasn't called me down on it yet. Maybe they haven't heard it—if they heard it, I'd hear from them."

Although there was no explicit threat of a lawsuit, she knew that she should not use legal terms like "case number" and "pending matter." Indeed, the whole call was intended to sound as if it came from a law office, and she carried it off very convincingly. It was a fine performance, and it worked; people did call her back, she said.

As we work through account after account, I express surprise that she, a top performer, is not getting more hits. I imagined she must succeed in extracting a payment on nearly every call. But even a top performer encounters a lot of frustration.

"It's like pulling the handle on a slot machine," Barbara said, indicating the account on her screen, where a blinking cursor highlighted the debtor's phone number. "You never know which one's going to hit."

Action Item: Fight Identity Theft

Often, people first become aware of identity theft when they receive a collection notice on an account they did not open. However, the collection agency presenting the demand for payment might be of little help in correcting the problem. You will need to contact the creditor, credit reporting agency, and the local police. For the steps to correct identity theft, see the Federal Trade Commission's Web site at www.ftc.gov/bcp/edu/microsites/idtheft/. For more information on disputing debts with collectors and stopping collection calls, see Chapter 20, "Stopping Collection Calls."

11

Strengths and Weaknesses

Sometimes, a debtor's circumstances have a special bearing on how their account will be treated. Toward the end of one week, I got a promise to pay from an Army noncommissioned officer in Arizona. He admitted to having been "young and foolish" when he ran up the credit card years before. Since then, the debt had dogged him, popping up each time he was stationed in a new location. My collection call, in fact, was the first "incoming" that he had received on this old debt since recently returning stateside, he said, adding that he had spent the past seven months in Iraq.

Whatever you think about the war, it is natural to feel gratitude, or at least sympathy, toward an individual soldier who has put his or her life at risk. That is not, however, the natural reaction of a debt collector. My coworkers know that military people have a special weakness that makes them easy targets. Servicemen and women may face difficulty advancing in their careers if their credit history is poor, especially if their duties require them to have security clearance.[1] Their creditors might even write a letter to their commanding officer, a "letter of indebtedness," to exert pressure to pay. A study by the Military Family Institute at Marywood University in 1997 found that the U.S. Navy alone processed more than 123,000 such letters annually.[2] Only direct creditors, not third-party collection agencies, are legally permitted to write such letters, but military personnel are not necessarily aware of this distinction. Certainly, my coworkers did not feel it was part of their job to explain the difference.

Looking at the soldier's credit report though, I realized that leverage was not on my side. The account I sought to collect was not listed on his report. The balance, more than seven years old, must have melted off his history. That meant it was also probably too late for the creditor to file a collection lawsuit, under the state's statute of limitations for unsecured debt.

The soldier seemed to be unaware of this information about his debt's status. I could either do the right thing—tell him—or do my job. Feeling uneasy, I gave him until the middle of the following week to call back with a plan for repayment, sending him "OTB," or out to borrow. This put off my decision of whether to tell him about the expired status of his debt. The fact that his credit report is clean, I reminded myself, does not remove his moral obligation to pay a just debt. Maybe he would even feel the same way, if he subscribes to an old-fashioned code of honor.

When I tell Pamela the situation at break, she seems amazed that I would even consider telling a willing payer that his debt had legally expired. It is a $1,200 balance, and our own jobs are on the line here, after all.

"Yeah, but the guy was in Iraq," I said—if, in fact, that part of his story was true. As it turns out, however, I am not forced to decide whether to tell the vet about his expired debt. The situation is resolved in the usual way when he fails to call back on the day we had set. Because I am continually reminded that suspicion and distrust are essential tools in this job, I wonder about the few marriages I know of between collectors. These are coworkers who met their spouse on the job and now work at different agencies, or even in the same building. Having extinguished trust in their professional life, can they still keep it alive in their personal life? Perhaps these unions work better than average. I imagine two collectors having no secrets from each other, disdaining falsehoods. But could a marriage—or even a friendship—survive the glare of complete honesty?

I do not consider myself a rube. Years of work as a newspaper reporter have given me a habit of healthy skepticism. I tend to roll my eyes at claims of good things that will happen in the future. But still, I am surprised at my gullibility on this job. I have been taken in by outright lies, whoppers delivered with all the seeming sincerity of a country preacher giving the Sunday sermon, and debtors who earnestly promise to call back, then disappear.

In this light, people who feel compelled to honor their debts begin to seem handicapped by their scruples. As much as I need to generate fee, there are accounts that I don't feel good about winning. Even though I'm not doing anything wrong, legally, my conscience gives me trouble.

One payment, a postdated check from a woman in Texas, was for the bed-wetting device, of all things. She was on Social Security and said she was struggling with cancer. But the device was for some other member of her family, she said, not very credibly. I felt a pang at her embarrassment and asked her what happened to the device. "Oh, we returned it all," she answered mildly.

"Well, there's a still a balance of $600," I said. Apparently, she did not make the return within the grace period, or perhaps she was hit with fees and financing charges. The account record does not contain much detail. "What do you intend to do?"

"Yes, we need to pay that," she replied. She had paid other bills with a postdated check over the phone before, indicating she had dealt with collectors. She knew where to find the routing number on her check, and gave the account number without being asked. The check was for $110 postdated to the end of the month, when her Social Security payment would arrive. If it bounces, I dread having to call her back and demand she make good. The Texas woman's check was my first payment for a two-week period. Small as it was, I was still eager to note it on the board, and hoped it was a trend toward bigger scores. My problem is closing with debtors. If they say they want a letter or more time, we set a date to talk again. Only I never hear from them again. One sincere New Mexico resident promised to pay in two days. When I called back, his phone had been turned off "at the customer's request," the phone company recording said.

I begin sometimes using a version of Barbara's message, modified to make it legally compliant—I hope. It is a notification that the call is supposedly being taped. All in the third person, it informs the "subject" that their file is under review and if they want to participate in the review, it will be necessary to contact our office, "for which purpose the following toll-free number is provided." Vague, but not threatening. I repeat the mini-Miranda warning, informing them that the call is an effort to collect a debt. I use the bored tone Barbara adopts, emphasizing that it is a legal disclosure. But I eschew a trick I have been taught, to hang up in the midst of the warning. "I am legally required to inform you that this is an attempt..." Click. The debtor hears that much and is intrigued. If the incomplete message draws a complaint, the collector can say that the connection was broken, or that the answering machine was faulty.

During one break, I chat with my fellow trainee Raymond and learn that he is starting a family; his girlfriend is pregnant. The couple moved here from the New York City area partly for the lower housing costs. Ray is a tall young man with red-rimmed eyes who tripped and fell spectacularly over a phone cord on our first day in Bart's classroom, minutes after we were lectured about workplace accidents. I remember how he glowed with embarrassment. We agreed the accounts weren't doing much for us. Less for him—he still has less than $100 in fee and we're nearly at the one-month mark. We have been warned that we need a minimum of $200 in fee by the end of the month to keep our jobs. He shrugged, saying he has some other things lined up. However, the fact that he's still here in the face of all the futile phone calling suggests otherwise. I feel bad for him, starting a family with only the wobbly support of a collection job. We count the people in our class who have dropped out. About half have quietly left, after not quite a month.

Then, we are suddenly reminded that there can be success amid all the failure.

"Say goodbye to Bobby," Gabe said to our training group. "Now you guys will get some work done." Bobby made his $2,500 in fee to graduate from training with a week to spare. He gathered up his stuff and carried it out to his new desk on the floor. Our resident "fraud investigator" made good. Aaron graduated too, but stayed at his old desk with us until they figured out where to put him. I asked how he did it, knowing how different his quiet style is from Bobby's aggressive and threatening talk-off. He shrugged and said, "I just slammed a lot of accounts." Meaning he kept dialing until he reached the willing payers and gave them a deal they could swallow—either a settlement or, more often, a monthly payment plan. I suspect that his personable nature, which makes him welcome at any table in the lunchroom, also helps him win over debtors.

I am at that time a long way from joining Bobby and Aaron. I train for an hour with another experienced collector on the floor who has a specific task of following up on the lapsed accounts of monthly payment plans. Danielle explained that once the accounts are six weeks behind on a payment, they are taken from the original collector, the one who set up the payment plan, and switched to her department.

None of the other pros out there would consent to let me sit with them at first. "I'll do it—grab a chair," she said brusquely. "Ah, I can't call him again," she said of the first account that appeared in her queue. The debtor lived in Pennsylvania. The compliance message that flashed on the screen said we can't call for a number of days after leaving a message. This was new information to me, having skipped through the compliance screens as fast as possible. I thought they were universally ignored, as had been the case during classroom training. We had learned to simply get them out of the way as fast as possible in order to see the account information and make the call. But Danielle scrupulously adhered to the rules, repeating the mini-Miranda warning on every message.

"Don't listen to him," she said of her male coworker on the other side of her divider, who was working straight credit card accounts from the general pool.

"Yeah," he agreed. "You'll get fired." The guy was doing the "legal talk-off," which is the opposite of lawful. On each call, he threatened debtors with unspecified legal trouble.

"What's your lawyer's phone number," I overheard him say. Then he continued, "You don't have a lawyer?" in a concerned tone. "Well, don't you think you are going to need one?"

The implied threat might generate complaints, but he explained that, as a floor collector who has a track record of making goal, he is protected from dismissal. That's when an important fact about the trainee group dawned on me—we are easily expendable. We may say wild, threatening things and, if caught on tape, the company has little invested in us.

"It's just a trainee; this doesn't reflect the organization; they're fired," management can say.

And that's that. We're cannon fodder. Indeed, a young woman trainee had been escorted out of the building during my first week on the job, after a complaint came in that was backed by an answering machine recording. For the agency, it is a "can't-lose" situation. If we use threats and they work, the agency gets revenue. If we're caught, the company has an easy out. No one will hold management's feet to the fire for the unauthorized remarks of a trainee with less than two months' experience. Yet, because the intake of trainees is so large, there are dozens of us working in the building at any given time. Our attrition is high from dropouts and terminations, but the slots are rapidly filled each week when Bart's classroom empties out. As a result, trainees make up a substantial portion of the overall workforce— about 20 percent I estimate, based on the space we take up inside the building and the throng of us outside, puffing on cigarettes during breaks. After training with Danielle, I return from the floor to my own desk seeing our training group in a different light. My growing sympathy for my coworkers rises another notch.

Back on the phone, I hold off on threats but try to find an advantage, as with this one debtor in a posh northern Virginia suburb. She had a good job and excellent credit; the one exception being the delinquent charge account that I was trying to collect. I had been leaving messages at her home and office for two weeks. No dice. She was wily enough not to come to the phone, letting her babysitter intercept the calls.

So, one morning I called her at 8:00 a.m. sharp, my first call of the day, hoping the babysitter hadn't arrived yet. It worked. The debtor made the mistake of picking up. "Yes, this is Melissa," she admitted. Her voice was, as I imagined, the smooth tone of an educated professional. I told her it looked like an oversight. Perhaps she had lost a bill, I said, tactfully not mentioning how she had ignored my earlier calls and used the innocent babysitter as a shield.

I'm working another debtor like that in Oregon, even ritzier. The bill is for $900 on a Neiman Marcus account. Her credit report is full of posh charge accounts like that, plus there are impressively large car and mortgage payments. But she's current on all of it, not a single one is behind, except the one I'm trying to collect. Her street address is something like Skyview Lane. I imagine her looking out at Mount Hood from a picture window as she intercepts my calls, picking up, and then hanging up the phone wordlessly. I can hear a moment of connection, a second of the air flowing past the receiver on her end, then the circuit breaks with a click.

After making a half-dozen of these calls—I put the account in my desk because of her great credit—I begin to picture her hand on the receiver, bony and tan, with a tennis bracelet dangling on her wrist. She doesn't work, I imagine. At least there's no employer listed on her credit report.

"I hate her," I tell a friend after work, laughing. But I am half serious.

"You don't know, maybe she has been sick, maybe she had a kid who got sick," my friend said, her motherly instincts kicking in.

"Well, if she did, it didn't show on her credit report," I reply. "There are no medical bills but plenty of spending."

I imagine the haughty matron went on a power trip and had a spat with some salesgirl at Neiman Marcus who wasn't sufficiently obsequious. Why else would she stiff that one charge account and not Nordstrom, Macy's, and all the others? If I get her on the phone and she waffles about paying, I'll bring up her Victoria's Secret account. A woman in her early 50s, she'll be embarrassed. I'm dying to hear her claim hardship, so I can ask why, if she was so strapped, was she charging up premium lingerie? Did that count as a necessity in her world? So I try her at 11:00 a.m. when the West Coast times in for us, but it is always the same—pick up, then click. Usually, I say her name in the second before the hang-up. Probably her answering machine is just full. She might be on an extended absence, sailing in the Caribbean or skiing the French Alps. But I prefer to imagine her hanging up on me wordlessly. It stokes my anger.

Payday reminds me of the gap between her economic status and mine. As usual, we stream out of the building to cash our checks at lunchtime. I drive with Gary to a nearby bar where they cash checks for a dollar, which is $6.50 less than the bank had charged us. This service is for customers only, so Gary gets me a Pepsi and orders a bourbon and Coke for himself. A group from my class sits munching hamburgers and downing beers—they had ordered ahead. They explained that they had quickly found the phone number on the Internet, after a search of our proprietary database failed. The lesson being, I guess, that it is getting easier for anyone to track down information, not just people with access to business-class database services.

The waitress finally came out of the back with a sheaf of bills, the pay for a bunch of guys. She must have had a few thousand dollars in cash back there in a safe. On the way back, Gary had me stop to get a

24-ouncer of vile-smelling malt liquor at the quick mart, which he consumed while we sat in the car in the parking lot, talking. "This won't get me drunk," he told me. "It just takes the edge off."

Working on Saturday, as we do at least once a month, makes me hope people will be home to answer my call. But a promise to pay (PTP) was all I got. It was no easier to reach debtors, and certainly no easier getting them to pay. The PTP was on a Sears card issued way back in 1986, now showing a $1,100 unpaid balance.

"We were making monthly payments, and they just sent this to some collection company," the debtor's wife said with sincere surprise.

I said it was a shame the creditor had simply terminated the long-standing account. The original lender had sold the debt; it was now held by a debt-buying company, which had farmed it out to us for collection. I had no way of knowing her payment history or financial situation because she lived in Vermont, the one state that forbids collectors from viewing debtors' credit reports. I offered an 80 percent settlement in three parts, the best I could do on that account. But she said it would be up to her spouse to nail down any agreement, and he was not there.

Action Item: Find Out If Your State Regulates Collectors

Many states license debt collectors and restrict their practices to a greater degree than the U.S. Fair Debt Collection Practices Act. To find out your state-level protections, contact the state attorney general's office or state consumer debt regulator. To locate your state attorney general's office, check the National Association of Attorneys General, whose Web address is www.naag.org. For listings of state-level debt collection regulators, contact the North American Collection Agency Regulatory Association (NACARA), whose Web address is www.nacara.info/. For more on state-level regulation, see Chapter 21, "Checking Out a Collector."

12

Collector of the Week

At the end of my fifth week, I reached another milestone. Near the end of shift, we were called down to the middle aisle for an impromptu huddle. Gabe looked at me and waved me down in particular as I stood up from the phone to see what was going on.

"This is about attendance, too," Mabel was explaining to the group, not just monetary performance. "OK, the collector of the week goes to..."

And she said my name. I had a feeling it might be me. Managers smile on my punctuality and work habits while they chew out my coworkers for being late and goofing off. I shot up my arms in a victory stance and nodded my head to the applause. As I walked up and took the envelope from Mabel's outstretched hand, I realized how this little ceremony was our version of the monthly bonus assembly that distributed real money out on the main collection floor.

"What'd they hook you up with, a gas card?" Ray asked. I tore open the envelope. "A $25 gift card to the mall," I said. "Not bad for just showing up."

"You're putting up fee too," he said. And it's true. At the end of five weeks, I have close to $900 in fee, meaning at least twice that in total collections. That's second best among my training class, which has dwindled to about half the original 20 people who showed up that first day over a month ago. Still, most of my total is from my three scores on one day, a day that is looking increasingly like an aberration.

"I'm so conflicted," I told a friend later. I didn't expect to do well in this job, being hypervigilant about obeying debtor protection laws. What's more, I'm concerned that my test of the effectiveness of a legally compliant collector might be skewed, as I bend toward some of the prevailing practices in the office. Most of my phone messages omit the problematic mini-Miranda disclosure. Legally, the full disclosure is required to be made only on the initial communication with the debtor, the collection law states, and the calls I make are never the initial contact. The notes appended to each account scroll back for screen after screen. All the way at the beginning is a notation that the debtor's initial notification letter has been sent.

After my moment of glory with the collector award, I follow up by missing most of the next week, including the end-of-month closeout push, because of a bad cold. I'm still coughing and sucking on lozenges when I return the next week. My throat is raspy, especially after a cup of machine coffee and a dozen phone messages. I switch to Red Bull, which is $2 a can from a machine in the hallway. It's cold and smooth and accomplishes the afternoon pick-me-up to carry me through quitting time.

While I was out, another crop of kids had emptied out of the classroom and riffled in among our desks. Now I am one of the old hands, having been in Part Two training for over a month. A guy in dreadlocks named Don plunks down in Benjamin's old stall; I show him how to put in the code for the new WIP (work in progress) when the digits are called out. While making his calls, he weaves from side to side in his seat and hums along to a private soundtrack playing in his head. A tall kid in his early 20s settles into the booth across from me, wearing a jersey with a pattern of hands clutching fistfuls of dollar bills. Both he and Don are acutely conscious of a third classmate of theirs, a willowy girl with a cascade of blonde-black curls falling past her thin shoulders, who sits further down the row.

These new trainees soon learn a lesson about the job as a piece of news races around the office: Bobby has been fired. He was caught sleeping at his desk, of all things. "His head was nodding," Gary says knowingly. Gabe acts unsurprised and uses the occasion as a teaching moment. "I told him, 'You'll last two weeks out there,'" he says. Making it out of Part Two training is no assurance of tenure. On the floor, everyone is quieter. They're more focused and performance-minded, Gabe says. In this tidy group, Bobby stood out like a weed. Some manager saw his clowning, his sporadic work habits, and took the first opportunity to bounce him out of the building with no appeal, no recourse. We learn later that he went directly to a collection agency down the street and was hired on the spot.

I must have left more than 2,000 phone messages by now, and still the phone startles me on the rare occasions when it actually rings with someone calling me back. The caller this time is a Louisiana man demanding the records from the MasterCard account that I said he owed.

"I never had a MasterCard, I only ever had a Visa, ever in my life,'" he says. He persists in calling me "sir," and wants the company to send him proof, a list of his supposed charges.

"I don't have that, just the balance and the date you signed the contract opening the account," I respond, still thinking the debt was genuine. "The card company seems to think you do owe this money."

But then I notice the address on the account is in a close-in suburb of New York City. When did he live in New York? For only two months in 2003, at the very time the credit card was issued, according to his credit report. According to him, never—he'd never dream of living in New York. "I've lived right here in this house for 35 years," he says proudly.

There the fraud sits, staring out at me on his otherwise pristine credit report. In this instance, it's pretty clear-cut. Someone used his name and identity to have a card mailed to them in New York, a place the debtor would not deign to visit. I document the account as disputed and do-not-call, shielding him from further dunning calls, at least from our agency. It will be up to him to get his credit report straightened out. He tells me the card issuer had contacted him once before and ignored his disavowal of the balance. "They sent a letter offering to settle for half of it," he says, disbelief in his voice. How could a responsible company ignore his protestations of fraud, his tone asks, and offer to bargain down the amount of the theft? How could a bank think of participating in someone's crime?

By the end of the call, the man was cordially thanking me for helping straighten out the records. There's some satisfaction in correcting a situation like that, but it's short lived. It happened that most of that day went similarly. There were no payers, only disputed debts. One woman said the bill was all her ex-husband's fault; and what wasn't his fault was interest, which was the card issuer's fault. Then, she said she wanted to use a debt consolidation company to deal with it. Consolidators are companies that offer to negotiate with creditors on your behalf. They claim to be able to wind up with a better settlement than you can achieve on your own. You send your payments to them, trusting that they will handle all the bills. We are coached to tell debtors that consolidators are scammers—which is true in some cases—and that they can get the best deal available from us directly, without some middleman.

Finally, when I pressed her to confirm her address for a follow-up letter, she hung up. In the same hour, a debtor told me her balance has been charged-off, as if that were the end of it. "Wasn't that charged-off?" she said. "I think that was charged-off."

"That doesn't mean the bank forgot about it," I said. "It doesn't mean they don't want their money back." Her comment echoed that of another debtor a few days earlier who recommended that the creditor had "better charge that off."

If there is a chance before these people hang up, I explain that a "charge-off" is an accounting term that indicates how the balance is treated on the bank's books. The creditor will place the account in "charge-off" status after a period of delinquency, usually 180 days. The status means the lender treats the amount as uncollectible for financial reporting and tax purposes. However, that's an accounting convention—it doesn't mean the creditor has given up on getting its money back. To the contrary, collection efforts will intensify as the creditor sends the account to collection agencies, sells it on the debt market, or even files a lawsuit to recover the balance. So, it is the height of wishful thinking to believe that a charged-off debt has been erased.

"I'm a blessed consumer advice bureau today," I said to Gary over the divider.

Friday brings the relief of a paycheck, and there's the usual swarm toward the exits at lunchtime. Gary cashed his check at the usual bar and downed a half-pint of Bacardi. It was obvious back at work. He didn't bother to leave messages and when he did reach someone, his voice was even louder than usual. He tried to leave an hour before quitting time, but Gabe caught him putting on his coat.

When Danny down the row starts making jokes about Gary's lunchtime beverage choice, Gary shows an ugly, dangerous side. Provoked, he reddens and seems to get even bigger, his massive shoulders hunching with stress. "You're talking stuff to management about me?" he says, following that up with a string of epithets.

"Everybody already knows about it," Danny protests. But this doesn't help calm Gary down at all. Danny is a glib talker, which makes him a natural in this business, but he can't squelch his squeaky voice at times when he should just shut up. The day before, during a conversation about the late comedian Richard Pryor, he got sidetracked and wound up explaining how to freebase cocaine. "The ammonia dissolves the cut; it takes out the cut and gives you more refined shit," he said, within earshot of Gabe and Mabel.

Not just our pod, but the entire trainee group seems to have had substantial experience with recreational drugs. One guy in my class who had to fill out the paperwork for ex-convicts on our first day is a "walking pharmacy," as Gary puts it, and a newer kid lets it be known that he's selling marijuana. He's not making many calls, he's making his contacts internally, Gary says. "He'll get canned and he'll only have to come back on paydays." Down the row, Willy, a pale kid in his mid-20s who looks even younger, is always on the lookout for Lortabs. Gary charged him $3 a pill for some spares that he had left over after dental work, the extraction of seven methamphetamine-ravaged teeth. I tell Gary that I don't understand the use of Lortabs as a recreational drug. "They make you not mind the passage of time," he explains.

I do, however, understand the need to alleviate the feeling of burnout from making call after futile call—I feel it, too. I think all of us have at one time or another. Without a payer, the days full of hang-ups and angry curses take a toll on the spirit. Solving disputes like that of the southern ID-theft victim provides only a brief respite. Nobody wants me to call; no one is glad to hear from me. Listening to the public radio station in the morning before work, I'm amazed by the activity during the pledge break. People actually call in, voluntarily putting $30, $60, or $100 on their credit cards. They seem to live in a different world than the bitter, grasping one that I inhabit. The people I speak to on the phone have already used up their credit card, long ago. The things they bought with it probably had more utility than the momentary good feeling of a charitable contribution—even if all they got was gas or groceries. Maybe there is a dividing line in the world. The people who phone in to give their money to a radio station are on one side; the people I call are on the other. That's probably an oversimplification, though. At least some of those flush, public-spirited contributors have since lost their jobs or run into some other kind of hard luck that forms the basis of their hard-luck story. Maybe the charge they made to the radio station is one of many now that sits on their used-up, burnt-out, charged-off credit card, and a collector like me is pestering them for the balance.

I made a deal with myself to let go of anger at the people who won't pay and appreciate the ones who do. Like one woman in a New York suburb who said she was waiting for someone to call at night, when she was home from work, because her stay-at-home husband doesn't know English. When he answers the phone, all he can say is "No hablo Ingles." To collectors, this means, "I am pretending not to know English." The willing payers are few and far between, but they are out there.

Gary and I discuss this as we share a ride home at day's end. He recounts how one elderly lady "beat him" because she made only a $100 down payment to start a monthly payment arrangement, when she owed $3,400. "Heck, take the hundred," I told him. "Don't get greedy. Look at me, wearing my dialing finger down to a nub, with hardly a dime to show for it all week. I'd be happy to pull in $100 on a $3,400 debt." It seems like a long time since my big Monday boosted my performance to the best in my training class.

In fact, we have been taught that building up a base of monthly payers, like the elderly woman Gary recruited, is how collectors survive in this business. The monthly payments provide a long-term, steady stream of revenue. If Gary's debtor stays on track, she'll be sending in $100 a month for nearly three years. As he continues to recruit other debtors into monthly arrangements, his fee sheet will fill in automatically. All he has to do is call these people four times a year, to get them to put another series of three postdated checks on file. By the end of a year or so, he could recruit so many regular payers that his monthly goal is met before he makes even a single call. Each new payment that he obtains will go toward his bonus. All this sounds great to Gary and me. In reality, though, we're both short-term thinkers, each in our separate ways. Disenchanted with the life of a debt collector, even a legally compliant one, I expect that I will decide to return to my job as a newspaper reporter at the end of my leave of absence.

It's snowing hard, leaving the road slick and treacherous. "At least it's not a whiteout," Gary says. For a California native who came to Buffalo via Las Vegas, he takes our northeastern weather in good stride. He explains that he's worked in worse.

"When I landed in Alaska one time, it was a whiteout. I usually like to look out and see the ground under me during landing. I was totally tweaked out, been doing meth for three days, totally spun. You get so paranoid. So, I look out and we're going down and there's nothing under the plane, I can't see anything but more white, and I'm like Arrrrrgh! This is it!"

He'd gone up there to work as a cook for a fish processing operation on an island off the coast. He was cooking for 250 people, mostly Filipinos who worked in the plant through the summer. "It was light all the time—you'd get out of work at 11:00 p.m., but it was broad daylight. Go out for a few drinks and before you know it, it was time to go back to work," he chuckled. "I lasted three months there."

He had got that job after having learned to cook in his family's delicatessen back in California. He was just a sandwich maker—a far cry from his high-earning, big-spending lifestyle in Vegas later on—but his face lights up with pleasure when he describes how people loved the meatball parmigiana subs he used to make, with their spicy morsels of ground beef tucked under a warm blanket of sauce and melted cheese. "That was nice," he said. "You made things for people, and people appreciated what you did."

Action Item: Protect Your Privacy

Collectors are forbidden from discussing your debt with people who do not share responsibility for the debt. Collectors may contact your neighbors, family members, or other "third parties," but only for specific reasons. For more on this restriction, see Chapter 22, "Using Collection Law."

13

Retention

As the onset of spring melts the mounds of snow in the parking lot into a slushy mess, we get a chance to work an entirely different sort of debt than we have been collecting up until now. One day, we are quickly huddled in the training room and given instructions on how to work "retention" business. Customer retention is very different work from the collections involving older, charged-off accounts. Once an account is charged off, the debtor is no longer a customer of the bank, but an adversary. By contrast, retention accounts are hovering in a limbo between healthy and defunct. Because they have missed one or more payments, the holders of these cards can't make further charges. It's not too late, however, to bring the card current. Just one payment will save the card from being closed out and going into charge-off status. Completing a series of six payments—which we call "buckets"—over six months will return the card to health, allowing charges to be made again.

The card issuer wants to avoid charging off the account, if at all possible, because then they can continue to charge interest on the balance, Julie explained. There might be provisions in the contract for post charge-off interest, but it's often much lower than the rate that can be charged on a live card. And, of course, there is the uncertainty of ever collecting it.

The rules for these accounts are odd. For one thing, the payments must be in the exact amount specified by the lender. Less, and the payment or "bucket" won't count. More, and the extra will go toward bringing down the balance, but won't bring the card back into usable status any faster. There must be six months of regular payments, each in the amount the lender specifies. Some of the buckets are a series of six equal payments, but some call for different monthly amounts. The biggest series I saw was six equal payments of $260. This was on a balance of five figures, so it doesn't take a large repayment of principal to keep a sizable balance in play.

Many of these retention accounts have substantial balances, and Julie tells us they're easier to collect for a few reasons—the main one being that the customers want to save the card. If the account is closed, the holder is immediately liable for the full balance, not merely a minimum monthly payment. In addition, we are permitted to say that, if they fail to make a payment, the account will be "sent to arbitration or litigation." That sounds like a harsher consequence than we can usually threaten—or legally threaten, at least. The phrase is allowed only in those exact words, she explains. "Because what are [the creditors] going to do after this—maybe send it to another collection agency, so that's a form of arbitration." If collection doesn't work, it could go to court. So the "or" in the phrase "arbitration or litigation" is critical. In actuality, these accounts once charged-off would be the sort we've been working all along, simply accounts in collections.

The accounts do at least come with solid, recent contact information on the debtors. However, they're inexplicably yanked away from us after just two hours. Without explanation, the WIP (work in progress) is turned off and we're given a different one, a grab bag of old, charged-off accounts from a debt buyer. To Gary, this is a sign of the decidedly nonmeritocratic nature of our workplace, a view he holds in contrast to my image of the company. Other favored departments, and even well-connected individuals, are receiving bigger, fresher, easier-to-collect accounts, he argues enviously. It is true that the better accounts are not awarded via democratic principles. I reply that the favored departments, which get fresher accounts, are populated by collectors who have proven themselves worthy.

Sometimes, a sign of favor can touch even a lowly trainee. I was feeling ready to quit one day when Tim, a group manager, appeared at my shoulder and changed my mind. He told me to work on accounts in his "desk," his group of accounts within the computer system. These accounts all had "PBK" status, for "promise broken." That made them hot prospects, he said. I puffed up a bit at this mark of favor, and at the opportunity to work supposedly lucrative accounts. I used a select command on Tim's accounts to cherry-pick the ones with good credit and substantial balances. There were a couple hundred of these, but they turned out not to be easy pickings. These people had broken their promises to pay because they had no intention of paying. Tim had selected me and one another guy in my class who was nearing graduation deadline to work them. If nothing else, it provided practice selecting accounts using the string of commands that the computer would recognize. You could look for a balance over $500, credit score over 500, unworked in at least three days, and other desirable characteristics. Established collectors, with 100 or more accounts in their desks, will use these select commands daily to prioritize their follow-up calls. But as for generating fee and getting me closer to graduation, these supposedly plum accounts proved to be dried out.

Action Item: Prioritize Your Debts

The bill being presented by a debt collector is probably not the most important one you face, despite what the collector might tell you. Pay essential bills first, including utilities, housing-related bills, and any child-support payments. Unsecured consumer debts, such as most credit card bills, have lower priority. For more on dealing with collectors' demands, see Chapter 25, "Negotiating a Debt Settlement."

14

A Complaint

"Fred, I don't care what debtors say," Mabel told me in an unusually mild tone, standing near my desk with her feet wide apart. "But I just want you to know that some woman called up and made a complaint about you."

I try to think who it might have been. Most debtors I reach are irate about being called and asked for money, even if they know they owe it.

"What did I do—ask her to pay a bill?" I said.

"That's probably it," Mabel replied.

"But you know me—I'm a pussycat."

She snorted. "Like I said, I don't care what debtors say."

That was the extent of my first and only complaint—at least the only one that I know about. If there had been a recording of me mistakenly saying something out of bounds, maybe it would have gone differently.

It is possible to run afoul of collection rules even when trying to be compliant. This is one claim of the collection industry that turned out, in my experience, to be true. More than once, I began discussing a debt with someone, after confirming their name matched that of the account holder, only to hear them say something like, "Oh, you want my dad, Dave senior." I had unwittingly violated Dave senior's privacy. Alternatively, they would claim not to be the debtor and say they misheard me when I asked for the debtor by name. Other times, incomplete account records make it difficult to confirm the debtor's identity.

I was collecting on overdrafts, which used to mean bounced checks, when I reached a young woman in New York City on her cell phone. She agreed to pay the overdue amount with her debit card. She had second thoughts, though, and authorization transferred her call back to me. She wanted to know what the bounced check was for, who it was made out to—information that I didn't have. It was a $219 balance, below the $500 threshold for ordering a credit report, which would have provided more information. The details on the account record were sparse.

"You have to admit, it's a bit shaky," she told me.

Although that might be true, I didn't have to admit it. She said she had been in Spain and was on a visit home, staying at a friend's house on the upper West Side. What I did not realize at the time was that many overdrafts now occur not on checks, but on debit card or ATM transactions that could have been turned down by the bank. Instead of stopping the transactions, banks have set up automatic "overdraft protection" programs that have turned customers' over-drafts into a source of profits.

"Should I talk to the bank about this?" the young woman asked.

"They've sent the account to us; you'll have trouble opening a new checking account as long as this is outstanding," I replied, using the one thing I did know to be true. "My advice is that you pay the bill." It was only $219 after all, representing about $30 in fee for the agency—not something I could spend the morning on.

Eventually we figured out what had happened. It had been New Year's Eve. She was abroad, and had used an old account with only a little money left in it to withdraw cash from an ATM. Apparently, the withdrawal had gone over the balance and triggered an overdraft fee. There was a settlement offer with a 20 percent discount available and I gave her that, although she was ready to pay the full amount.

The easy payment, however, was a rarity. Even though overdrafts aren't supposed to be lines of credit, debtors frequently complained that the bank was bleeding them for these mistakes, tacking on high fees for small errors.

"They got me; they got me so bad," said one fast-talking man in upstate New York. "I was over by one dollar—one dollar—and they charged me all this." His account said he owed the bank about $240 for the overdraft. So, according to his story, the bank had tacked on $239 in overdraft fees.

In the time since I quit working as a debt collector, federal regulators have changed rules governing overdrafts, protecting consumers from at least some of the fees that had previously been common. Toward the end of 2009, the Federal Reserve issued a rule that banks must stop assessing fees for overdraft services, which cover overdrafts on ATM use, unless the account holder affirmatively agrees to the service, or "opts in."[1] For accounts in collection, these sorts of fees have been added to accounts that the consumer had emptied and abandoned. Other consumers pay the overdraft charges to keep the account open.

The Fed's move came as attention focused on how overdraft fees and related policies have quietly become a profit center for banks. A 2009 report by the Center for Responsible Lending found that bank overdraft fees had increased 35 percent in two years, reaching $24 billion the year before.[2] Some banks are amending their practices. Bank of America said it is dropping the practice of allowing ATM transactions to go through without sufficient funds to cover the debit.[3]

Some of the overdrafts I tried to collect were greater than $1,000, which seemed unlikely to be entirely the result of fees. One New York City man argued that he wasn't responsible for the $1,000-plus overdraft because he had closed his account before an automatic payment was scheduled to be withdrawn from it. "How can they charge me for an account I closed, tell me that," he demanded. It came out that he closed the account in an effort to evade a court-ordered obligation resulting from a less-than-amicable divorce.

Usually such court-ordered payments are top priority for consumers. They put their old credit card debts at the end of the line—where they belong.

"I'm paying other things," one debtor told me. "I have to make child-support payments—I could go to jail if I miss that, so that's more of a priority." I offered to erase 20 percent of the balance, but he had heard of settlements as deep as 50 percent, and figured he would wait for a deal like that. I did not tell him that I'd heard of those deals too, but they were being offered by a different bank than the one that issued his credit card. Nor did I try to frighten him with the possibility of nebulous consequences if he didn't pay voluntarily. If he was facing jail on other obligations, nothing I could say would sound terribly frightening.

He was probably right that waiting would do him no further harm because his account was already in charge-off status and the black mark was already on his credit report. But, in general, before that point, waiting to pay a delinquent balance probably won't make things any better. Time is not on your side with a credit card. This holds true whether you're behind in payments or not. Suppose that you start with a zero balance and pay off your new charges during the grace period that most cards allow before interest begins to accrue. You actually come out ahead of the game. You get the use of the money during the grace period interest-free. Furthermore, on some cards, you rack up points toward frequent flier miles or other perks. It even looks good on your credit report. You have an open line of credit and by using it responsibly—taking advantage of the bank, in effect—you actually get a gold star from the financial industry.

If you make only the minimum payment, however, you'll be paying interest on the charges for years. Miss a payment or two and things get worse. The penalty interest begins to kick in, plus the late fee. Soon you're paying mostly interest and only whittling down the charges you made earlier. Stop making those payments and eventually your account is in charge-off status, where things deteriorate further. Interest may continue to be added, your credit report is tarred and feathered, and your account is sent out to a bunch of bill collectors whose job depends on extracting money from you however they can.

Even that might not be the end of it. On some credit reports, I have seen court judgments for little more than a $1,000 balance. The report doesn't show how much in legal fees, court costs, and other fees were tacked on to the original debt. Nor does it indicate if the judgment was collected through an embarrassing and financially grueling garnishment of the debtor's wages. To a credit card issuer, time is money alright—your money.

Action Item: Lodge a Complaint

If you have been harassed or misled by a debt collector, you can file a complaint under federal law and perhaps state law as well. Making a formal complaint might help rein in practices of noncompliant collection agencies. To make a complaint to the U.S. Federal Trade Commission's Consumer Protection Bureau, contact the FTC or go to its Web site at https://www.ftccomplaintassistant.gov/. For more on complaints, see Chapter 20, "Stopping Collection Calls."

15

Data Minefield

One day at lunchtime, I offered Gary a ride to the supermarket to combine our weekly shopping. He had been talking all morning about food his family's deli used to make—meatball subs, chicken parmigiana—and it was making me hungry. He bought a pair of crab cakes out of the seafood case and put them on white bread for his own lunch, squirted with mayonnaise packets he had picked up somewhere. He also got a six-pack and punched down two beers in the parking lot while we ate. One I watched him pour right down his throat without stopping, his thick neck bulging with each swallow and the tip of his tongue protruding slightly. He hunched forward so he could tip the can all the way up for the last mouthful. It turned out that it was his sister's family who had the deli. His own family operated a different business.

"My dad was pure Sicilian, one of those gangsters," he said. "He had a couple arrests for dealing drugs, did time in jail."

"So you're connected."

"He's connected; I'm not."

Gary explains that he is on the outs with the dad, who is disappointed in how he turned out. "What's that?" I reply. "Your convict dad is disappointed at how you've turned out?" At least Gary doesn't have a rap sheet.

"He wanted me to be everything he wasn't," my friend says. During the drive back to work, we discuss the link between genes and behavior.

Returning to my desk, one coworker asks if I am about to graduate. I tell him I'm still $500 short in fee. My projected graduation is the coming Friday, but I've only brought in $2,000.

"Oh, you know they'll give it to you," he said.

It's true that taking into consideration all the fee that will be coming from my payers in postdated checks, later this month and in coming months, my fee will surpass $2,500. However, the future payments are not credited until they're in the office.

This exchange occurs as we wait in the hall behind a cluster of dark-suited executives. These are clients of our agency who stand talking together in the hallway, causing a backup all the way to the stairs. All of us tough collectors stand meekly, waiting for the suits to notice us milling around behind them. We had been told that clients were in the building that day, from a prominent bank in New York that issues credit cards among its global operations, and to behave appropriately. "Don't put on your hats until you're outside," Mabel had ordered at the beginning of lunch break. These clients are people whom I want to interview as a reporter, but have never managed to break through their wall of gatekeepers and spokespeople. Do they spend enough time on collection floors like this to know what really goes on? How much emphasis do they put on compliance? Are they aware that "compliance" is a euphemism for not getting caught? We know enough not to shout threats into our phones when the word goes out that clients are on the floor, but they would have to be idiots to think they're seeing an unvarnished version of the place.

In a sign of my potential continued employment, I'm scheduled for a human resources meeting to hear about the benefits that will be available after three months on the job. Then, I discover that others who are further behind in fee than me are scheduled for the same meeting. As it turns out, however, I miss almost the entire thing while I talk with a hot prospect, a California woman named Crystal who owes $3,200. The fee on this single account could fulfill my goal and save my job.

I had reached her the previous week and set up a promise to talk again. She said she wanted to download her credit report to verify the debt, the card having been shut off years previously. When she actually calls back at the appointed time, I take it as an excellent sign, and skip my meeting to talk to her. I think I have hooked her with the prospect of a 50 percent settlement on the balance, although she says that she'd like to get it down to $1,000. She said the credit limit on that card had originally been $1,200.

I told her the 50 percent settlement was the best we could do. "If they take less than half, realistically, why would they bother to collect at all," I said. That will wipe out a lot of the interest. "There'll still be some, but this account hasn't been paid for a few years, so I think that's fair."

Eventually, she agreed and said she would ask her mother for a loan to make the settlement. If that falls through, she says she'll start a monthly payment arrangement. She managed to convince me of her sincerity by calling back and updating her contact information, including a work number. The performance is so convincing that I have forgotten the cardinal rule of promises: They are free to make in unlimited quantities. Any commodity that cheap must have very little value. There's only one sure sign of a debtor's willingness to pay—a good-faith payment.

I have an extra reason to worry that Crystal will not bother to pay: Her debt is about to expire. State laws set an expiration on unsecured debts, with some exceptions for things like taxes. In most states, the expiration is between three and ten years, with the typical period being six years. This is separate from the seven-year time limit for negative information appearing on your credit report. The statute of limitations on unsecured debt means that creditors can no longer file a lawsuit to recover after the legal clock has run out. However, this rule is fraught with complications. One involves the date when the limitation clock starts. This is usually the date of "last activity" on the account, which can itself be open to dispute. Another complication involves choosing the state whose rules should apply to the account, if you have moved to a state other than the one where the account was opened.

The collection industry's term for expired debt is "out-of-stat." Another widely used term for this kind of debt is "time-barred" debt. However, these are terms that my fellow trainees and I have not heard in class or read in our manuals. The statute of limitations is a fundamental part of the collection business if you are buying or selling accounts, or trying to run an agency profitably. For collectors, however, it's unhelpful—something we're better off not knowing. Because we're not threatening legal action anyway—at least, that is our cover story—the statute of limitations is not officially a factor. We're just trying to convince people to pay their debts voluntarily, after all. Not being involved in the legal end of things, we can sail right on past the six-year mark and keep on demanding payment, presumably on moral grounds. The statute does not limit attempts to collect a debt after the deadline, only legal actions to collect. Those collectors who use threats of lawsuits as part of their talk-off will keep right on making them, erroneously as well as illegally. Although many debtors know that debts will vanish from their credit report, most are unaware that their debts also have a legal expiration date. If we were taught about it, or if account records were built to reflect the statute expiration, we would be in a position of withholding the information. Management deceives us, or at least withholds information about the weakness of older debts, so that we may better deceive debtors.

As a reporter, I would shake my head at this practice; but as a collector, I see the wisdom of not making our jobs any harder than they already are.

Action Item: Find Out If Your Debt Has Legally Expired

Unsecured debts are subject to a statute of limitations under state laws, meaning that creditors can no longer sue you to collect after a designated period. Typically, debt not backed by property expires from three to ten years after its due date. However, this depends on the state, the type of debt, and whether any payments have been made since the initial delinquency. Check with your state Attorney General's office at www.naag.org to determine the rules in your state. To learn more about checking the status of your debts, see Chapter 23, "Reading Your Credit Reports."

16

Graduation Day

On a Friday, I reach my projected graduation date, the two-month mark since being hired. The day by which I was supposed to have collected $2,500 in fee, I start the day $500 short. The late shift the night before left me low on sleep and jacked up on coffee. I get some more caffeine at the gas station on the way in with Gary. He gets a cup also to wash down some Lortabs, to dull the pain from his tooth extractions. He is determined to get through the hours of work and pick up his paycheck, it being payday.

"Don't bother postdating," Julie says in the morning huddle. The major credit card accounts that we are working are about to be pulled back by the creditor. Nothing will count after the end of the week. The credit card issuer will bundle all these thousands of accounts and sell them on the debt market, she says. Good luck to the poor souls who get them after us and try to squeeze something out of them.

Tim taps me on the shoulder to go into his file. So I churn through that in the morning, popping up names that were already familiar. Some I'd had contact with. One woman works at a nearby collection "law office," one of the imitators of the Lenahan Law Office. I get her kid to bring her to the phone, hearing her grousing the whole way. Of course, she hangs up as soon as I state my business. I don't bother to call back. How could I intimidate one of those people? She wasn't necessarily a collector, but she must know the ropes.

By midafternoon, I am sick of the picked-over, broken-promise files, having become familiar with the names of the debtors and their reasons for nonpayment. It seems like an overwhelming effort to come up with something new to say. What's more, calling accounts from a variety of different creditors makes it impossible to get a rhythm. It's necessary to check first where the account originated, to avoid being dumbstruck when a live debtor answers. "Oh, hello, what am I calling about, you ask? Good question. Looks like a credit card of some sort, or a store account from Best Buy or Lowes or Wal-Mart. Or perhaps it's an overdraft—have you bounced any checks lately?"

So I drop Tim's prospects and go into the file of credit card accounts that most trainees are working, remembering the 43 percent commission rate they carry and my few early successes with them on that one Monday, so long ago now, when I got three payers.

On almost the first call, I get a woman debtor on the line. She tells me she is refinancing her house and using the proceeds to pay off all her outstanding obligations. Flustered, I look through the file. There was no promise to pay on this account. It was a $2,200 balance, the card having been closed in 2002. She mentions a much larger balance that she has already arranged to pay with my company with her home equity proceeds. However, she is aware of the card I am collecting on, saying she assumed it was in her settlement deal.

Well the problem is, those settlements are about to expire, I tell her. Unless we lock in the settlement today, these accounts are all being recalled by the creditor. She says that the bank lending her the home equity money will make up the payoff checks. I explain how we don't take checks by regular mail, but over the phone. Does she have her checkbook? She does. So I calmly start typing in the 50 percent settlement—the commission on which will boost my total to the $2,500 goal needed for graduation, or close enough to it.

Then, a hitch appears. "Check over $1,000 requires manager approval," the screen blinks. Shoot—I call out for Mabel. She jogs out of the room to get a higher-up's signature while I stall. I joke with the debtor while making a show of updating her contact information. "Best time to call—how about 'never,' does 'never' work for you?" She laughs and says that is the whole idea. Mabel comes back with an approval code. I input that, then the check routing number and the account, and postdate it to the end of the month. Once that notation is made on the account, I transfer her to the authorization department and put the phone down.

I made it.

"Yo everybody, Fred just got a payment for $1,000!" Mabel tells the room, giving the approximate figure. "Give it up." I get backslaps and high fives as I walk to the whiteboard to post the payment. "That will get you outta here," Mabel says, meaning I will graduate training and consequently keep my job.

But I return to my desk with a sense not of victory, but foreboding; expecting some problem to strike that will cancel the payment. Maybe authorization will call back with a problem concerning the debtor's check. But the phone is silent. Gary is standing up, beaming at me. "You're outta here!" he says, his meaty hand enveloping mine as we shake. He asks about the account and I tell him how the payment just fell into my lap. No argument, no threats; the debtor was ready and willing to pay. As we tell each other, these ripe accounts do exist, ready to pour out money like a slot machine that's primed to hit the jackpot.

Beginning to settle down, I pull my headset over my ear and position the microphone in preparation for my next call, when I hear Julie call my name.

Big problem: The postdate is for the thirty-first, a week after all the credit card accounts are to be pulled from our office. Hadn't I listened that morning in the huddle? The check is no good, she says. Get the money in sooner. So, I call the debtor back, apologetic, trying to get her to postdate for the 25th or even the 28th, when the money would actually clear her account. No dice. Her home equity loan won't close until the end of the month, she says. She can't write checks before that.

As pumped as I was about the payment, I am even more deflated when I see it fall through—as I'd somehow known it would. I leave it in Julie's and Mabel's hands to see what they can work out. Hopefully, the postdated check on file will allow us to keep this one account from being recalled with all the hundreds of others.

Gary is crestfallen on my behalf, saying how it was not my fault. In any other situation, a postdate for the end of the month would be fine. Then I get a reprieve. As I walk back from the whiteboard where I erased my score, Tim tells me that he will count the payment toward my goal for graduation purposes; the logic being that the payment would count under normal circumstances.

I thank him, feeling uneasy about the charity. It seems clear they want to give me a mulligan, even though I'm short of goal. "I have every confidence in you that you'll make it, Fred," Mabel says to me on the way out.

On the same day, my classmate Harold, one of the 20 who started training with me in Bart's classroom that cold day in January, was fired—no special treatment for him. I heard about it from the office gossip. Only five of us from that group are still at the agency, counting the two who went right to the floor because of their previous collection experience.

Disappointment followed disappointment. Crystal, the prospect in California who seemed so sincere about paying the previous week, failed to call at the time we had arranged. I called the workplace number she had given me. "Crystal hasn't worked here for three months," they told me. I called her cell and left a voice mail, stinging with the humiliation of being deceived. I indulged in a fantasy of her calling back next week sometime. "Your account number?" I would say coolly, pretending not to recognize her name. Politely, I'd tell her that the settlement offer had regrettably expired.

So it goes in my daydreams. In real life, I know I will have to swallow my pride and try to hold her to the promise she made, if I ever get her on the phone again. This is the point at which it's tempting to unleash the threat of legal action. Having already given the maximum settlement, there's no other inducement I can offer.

Recounting my roller coaster of a day to a friend after work, I reflect on how far I have drifted away from the consumer's point of view. Now that I'm struggling to keep my job as a collector, consumer protection seems like part of a different world. Most of the consumers I deal with are quite capable of protecting themselves. What about the credit card payer, my friend asks, the one who's refinancing her house to pay off an unsecured debt? Here she was, taking equity out of her house to pay a bill—one stuffed with penalty interest and fees—that was nearly old enough to disappear from her credit report. "Just as a person," my friend asked, "didn't you want to tell her?" The truth? No. God no! This was my ticket to the floor, my reprieve from the training group. This payment would save me from dismissal. More than that, it was my demonstration that I could do this job, that I had what it took, that I was as good as Aaron and Bobby, and the others who had surpassed me in fee. This, a big account with a juicy fee landing on the last day of my training period, would keep me from being a washout. Somehow, my performance as a collector had become important to me. After only a couple of months, I had adopted the mind-set of a professional collector. Even though it's not a job I expect to keep, I feel compelled to earn fee to keep up with my peers. I try to imagine how much more pressure they feel, needing the job and the paycheck to live on.

I noticed only recently that the names of last year's top-performing collectors are emblazoned on a banner that stretches the length of the big room, the floor where collectors work. I can hardly see it up there on the wall, though I walk under it every day, on my way in and out of the building. I have rarely walked out into the big room to take in the view; only during one-on-one training with a floor collector like Barbara. It's not my place.

Action Item: Bargain Down Your Debt

Debt collectors might be willing to accept partial payment to settle your debt instead of demanding the full amount. If you are able to complete the settlement payment within one to three months, a substantial discount on the full balance might be available. For a full discussion of negotiating a debt settlement, see Chapter 25, "Negotiating a Debt Settlement."

17

On the Floor

The following workday, while the car radio recounted the fallout from an ominous collapse on Wall Street, Gary told me about a financial debacle of his own.

"You won't believe what happened to me," he said as he settled into the passenger seat for the ride to work. "I got robbed last night—they got $850."

He was drinking with another guy from his halfway house when they got mugged, sometime after midnight. One of the robbers hit him over the head with a bottle or something and knocked him out. An ambulance took him to the hospital where they stitched him up. He ended up walking home, sometime before dawn. He seemed calm and resigned in my car on our way to work. He was right; I didn't entirely believe it. It was difficult to ask for too many details without seeming to doubt his story. Like why he was carrying every penny he had in the world in his pocket, in cash—his two-weeks' pay plus the money he got for selling his Civic, which he can't drive because of a suspended license.

At work, he got a hard-boiled brand of sympathy. "Well, Gary," Mabel said after she heard the story, "I feel bad for you. Are you ready to go back to Vegas now?"

My luck was different than Gary's. I tried to sign in, but my name wasn't on the list. "Because we love you," Mabel said. "You're outta here." Before an hour was up, Julie came around to my desk.

"Here, please sign this," she said, handing me a certificate. Completion of Part Two, it read. Identical to the paper I received after getting out of Bart's classroom two months ago, except for the number. I asked if the big credit card account I scored had been saved from being returned to the creditor.

"You got a few gifts," she explained, with an exaggerated wink. I checked my "desk," the accounts designated for me, and found two payers I'd never seen before. Tim had sent them to my area and inserted a note that their fee was credited to me "as per incentive." I checked the notes and saw that I had never called either of these people. I didn't recognize the initials of the collectors who had worked these accounts, so they were probably folks who had washed out of training earlier for some reason. There goes my picture of the collection floor as a pure meritocracy, where ability is the only thing that counts. It appears that my shortfall in fee is being overlooked because of my steady work habits; presumably, they will pay off eventually. Beyond that, am I getting special treatment because of my past experience? I don't see any indication of that. If my past work as a journalist were under consideration, I think they'd find a way to fire me rather than advance me—it would be just as easy, if not easier. There was the complaint Mabel had received, the details of which she hadn't bothered to tell me. That could easily have been trumped up into grounds for dismissal or my unexcused three days' absence with a cold.

Tired as he was, Gary sounded almost blasé as he talked-off a debtor into a $6,000 settlement on a $10,000 balance. Very calmly, he asked if the guy had a check on him because we needed the routing number. No? Did he have a canceled check somewhere? Gary seemed to have almost reeled in the payment, and I felt bad for him as I saw it slip away. Eventually, the debtor hung up.

"I'll never hear from him again," Gary said with a sigh. At lunch, he came with me to the post office just so he could nap in my car. He had not slept much the previous night, even if you count the period following the robbery when he was unconscious. I woke him at the drive-through and asked if he wanted a sandwich, to help me celebrate my graduation. Gary ordered two double cheeseburgers from the dollar menu, keeping his tab low.

"This has been the worst day of my life," he said toward the end of our shift.

"You mean, your life so far," I replied, imitating Mabel's brand of keep-your-chin-up sympathy.

My day had not gone well either; I collected no money, only a couple of promises. One guy on his cell phone said he was driving and couldn't talk. "I tried to call [the creditor] and set something up to pay," he said, "and they told me they'd sent the account to some collection company."

"That would be us," I said.

"And that someone would be getting in touch..."

"That would be me." The debtor seemed sincere about starting a monthly payment arrangement before the end of the month, but I was never able to get him to answer his phone again, driving or stationary.

The next day at the beginning of my shift, Julie came over to my desk. "Get your stuff together," she said, "I'm taking you over."

I pulled thumbtacks out of the fabric-covered particle board and gathered my papers, the unused message script with its yellow streaks of highlighter, while my coworkers spoke into their phones. I had received the high fives the other day when the news came down; now it was back to business. I looked around—there was no one left from when I'd started. Benjamin had quit, Aaron and Bobby had moved on; Joe was long since fired. Each of the desks across from me had housed two or three new occupants in the weeks since I had come out of Bart's classroom. I had stopped bothering to remember the names of the newest trainees.

"You're going to the mixed purchase department," Julie said, leading me on a hike to the corner of the building diagonally opposite from my desk in training. The manager there was Stewart, a guy about 15 years younger than I am.

"S'up," he greeted me. Stew put me in an empty stall directly behind his desk and told me to see him when I got settled. I got the broken phone going, to an extent, put my cheat sheets up and went over.

The department was aptly named. Stew explained the mix of stuff I'd be working—there were six different works in progress (WIPs). Along with the usual credit card charge-offs, there were some tax refund loans that went sour, unsecured personal loans that the lenders must have been bonkers to have written in the first place, and store charge accounts, many from Home Depot. One of the WIPs is prelegal, he said, meaning the creditor will send the account to court as their next step, if we don't get the money. This means that we can legally threaten the debtors with a lawsuit if they refuse to pay, he explains. This strikes me as a convenient arrangement for us and for the creditor.

"Work the Home Depot; it's sweet stuff," Stew urges. "All these people are homeowners, right? Who else goes to Home Depot?"

Who else? Penniless building contractors, that's who. This becomes clear during the first hour of work. The debtor profile is that of an independent guy-with-a-pickup-truck. These handymen have used the store's charge account with gusto. It's probably the only loan they can get, and maybe their only capital. Theirs is a business on a shoestring and when the string snaps, the charge account goes unpaid. That is, if their business was really a business at all, and not some home-improvement scam. These entrepreneurs are ducking and weaving like Ali. The account record contains their "office number," usually a cell phone. Their reluctance to answer it says much about the state of their business.

Stew divides the work up into two main WIPs. You work the first one until you get a payment that day. Then, you can work the second, which has better debtor profiles—more available credit, a mortgage showing, and so forth. So the deal is, you do what is necessary to get a hit on the beaten-down accounts, so you can work the slightly better ones.

The floor—this was it, what I had been working toward for the past two months. Still, it wasn't a good feeling to have graduated to the big room. Our small department with its grab bag of accounts felt like a step backward. Other departments will work one debtor exclusively, or a certain type of account, like auto deficiencies. The word about the mixed purchase department is that the accounts are just as bad as those in training.

Stew chirps cheerleading phrases every few minutes that are supposed to be motivational, and speaks with the same hip-hop slang used by the youngest collectors.

"How much do ya love me?" he asked Evan, the guy sitting next to me, at one point.

"A lot," was the laughing reply. Stew had credited Evan for a fee on an account he'd worked before it had gone to the attorney settlement department. Once a debtor refers us to his lawyer, we kick the account to a special department that takes things from there. I assume that this attorney settlement department is one place in the building where compliance with consumer protection law is taken seriously.

Worse than the difficult accounts in the mixed purchase department was my sudden transformation from an experienced person into a newbie, a greenhorn who had to depend on his new pod mates for embarrassingly basic information. "What's your phone number here?" I had to ask, the toll-free callback number being different from the one used in the training department.

At our late-afternoon dinner break on one evening's shift, I drive Gary to another collection agency where he can pick up a $200 check. He's earned the money for connecting this start-up agency with his brother-in-law, a debt broker back in California, who has supplied them with accounts. The new agency is housed in a converted Masonic temple that resembles a church. The office is on the second floor, which has been added to the building by bisecting the navelike room horizontally. The ground floor houses a women-only gym. Upstairs, the familiar cubicle arrangement and whiteboard are laid out incongruously under a vaulted ceiling.

"We've been going for a year, 18 months," explains the blue-suited manager who meets Gary and me. "Mostly just setting up. Getting licensed. A hundred thousand dollars later," he says, his voice trailing off. Only recently have they been able to start collection work in earnest, he said. Back at our office, Stew leaves at five o'clock and I begin to settle in. There are fewer people in the pod and less tension. Behind me, Marisol fires Spanish into her phone like a Gatling gun. I ask her to talk to a Spanish-speaking debtor for me at one point. She graciously says she'll work people for me, as long as they have decent credit and a balance worth the trouble. "I won't take trash," she said.

On a Wednesday, my first full day in the department, Stew announced he would let everybody into the good stuff, a special WIP, because it was closeout. "This board's not looking good," he said. "C'mon people, we need to pull it together and get this done. I need $6,000 to make my goal."

Unit managers are under the same pressure as collectors, with monthly goals divided into daily averages. They balance a combination of goading and helping collectors to produce. Young and green, Stew's attempts at psychological manipulation are transparent. "Thank you, everybody—I know you all have been pushing; thank you for your work. Now it's closeout..." he began the morning's pep talk.

The larger department of which the mixed purchase department is a part will receive a company-paid happy hour if we hit 100 percent of goal; it was written on the board. A new goal sheet came out. Now my monthly goal has bumped up to $4,500, from the $2,500 needed to exit training.

On the floor, we use an automated dialer to ratchet up productivity. It works great—it enrages people twice as fast as manual dialing. Anyone who's received an automated call knows how irritating it is to pick up and find a robot on the other end. The irritation is compounded when the robot is calling from a collection agency. An automated voice calls the primary phone number on an account. "If you wish to talk to an associate about this matter, press 1," it says. This screens all the no-answers and answering machines that a collection worker would normally have to plow through. The dialer detects an answering machine pickup, and the robot leaves a standard message. We only get involved if a person answers and elects to speak with us.

However, the person waiting on the line is rarely the debtor. Most are people hotly demanding that their number be removed from our records. I'd be angry too if some auto-dialer kept ringing my home phone, looking for someone else.

Then again, even when we reach the correct person, they are rarely glad to hear from us. One guy being dunned for $61 on a tax loan delinquency demanded to know how I could be so stupid as to try to collect on a bill that was already on his credit report. He seemed to think that that canceled the obligation, and hung up before I could explain that paying the bill would help his credit.

An elderly man returning a call demanded to know what the issue was that the auto-dialer's message referred to. "Do you have the reference number?" I asked. Yes, he said he did, but I should be able to tell him what the issue was first. "Well, without retrieving the records, I don't know what the issue is," I said. "That's why we leave that reference number with the message." I can't reveal that this is a collection call until the person confirms they are the debtor on the account. However, this caller decided that my reticence meant I was a scammer and started dumping invective on me by the shovelful.

Some people try to exact revenge for their inconvenience by turning the situation around on me. As I was preparing to leave for the day, a woman called back and gave a name that matched the one on the account record. She said she had already paid off the bill and asked me to wait while she looked up her receipt. After several minutes, I asked her to fax her documentation to us instead. She snapped, demanding to speak to the manager. By not waiting for her, I was harassing her, she said, and threatened to file a complaint with the state attorney general.

"If I wasn't picking you up in the morning," I told Gary on the way home, "I would have quit, a bunch of times. You saved my job at least five times." He laughed. He plans to leave the agency after he saves up some cash from his wages. He has graduated out of training to the auto deficiencies department, but the going is tough. The balances are large, but the debtors are unwilling to pay, having already seen their car repossessed; they feel they have suffered enough. Gary has lost hope of making his monthly goal, much less of reaching the elite group of five-figure bonus earners.

"I called my dad, said I'm coming home to Cali," Gary tells me. If he comes back "right," with a few thousand bucks saved, his dad will probably help him out.

I do learn one thing on the main collection floor that makes me glad I stuck with the job this long. The question about the compliance department's role in the operation becomes more clear one day. I had wondered just what this department's job was, given the widespread and frequent use of outlaw collection tactics throughout the building.

"Latisha, compliance is on you," Stew says at one point during a long afternoon of dialing. "Work five accounts." She started to ask a question but Stew cut her off. "Just work five accounts." He didn't want to have a lengthy discussion about it. He gave her no special instructions about how to work them, but his message was clear. She knew what not to say on those five accounts.

I couldn't tell how he knew that Latisha's line was being monitored. It seemed that he referred to his phone, a console unit with blinking lights indicating the lines in use. It wasn't the only time this happened. At least once a day, I heard him warn individual collectors when their calls were being monitored.

In this way, the "audit" tapes that the compliance department collects should portray a rigorously lawful operation, with fully compliant and even gracious collectors. Clients, the creditors who hear these recordings, will have a false picture of our operation, as will industry regulators, if they ever get their hands on the tapes.

My reporting on other agencies has indicated that companies are capable of cooking up stories. Even in court, the company might continue to make denials, not always truthfully. In 2003, Pennsylvania resident Nadine Frankenfield sued an agency in New York State for what she claimed was harassment. While she lay at home trying to recover from lung cancer surgery, the collectors called her repeatedly, ignoring her pleas to stop. Sometimes they would call multiple times in a single hour, she said, just to disturb her. The company denied it when she complained, and continued its denials when her lawyer took the case to court.[1] The company provided copies of its phone records that showed a legally compliant pattern of calls, with no more than one call on any given day.

Normally those denials, supported by company records, would be enough to stymie a complaint. But Frankenfield's lawyer thought the agency was lying and found a way to push the case. Through the discovery process, he subpoenaed call records from the telephone company itself. The official telephone company records, from what was then Bell Atlantic, showed a very different picture than the records that the agency had given the court. On a single day, for example, the agency had made multiple calls, one minute after the next, to Frankenfield's number.[2] The company eventually settled the case for an undisclosed sum and Frankenfield's estate—she died before the conclusion of the case—received the payment. The erroneous phone records that the company supplied were buried in case files in the federal courthouse. Having settled, the company could claim that no wrongdoing had been proven. Its official record remained unblemished.[3]

As I had feared it would, the $1,100 credit card payoff, the one that got me out of training, fell through. The debtor called, gave her account number, and said that her loan was scheduled to close on the third of next month, not the end of the current month. She insisted that I cancel the postdated check she had authorized.

Stewart at first said to do nothing. That would let the check bounce, most likely. The unstated plan was to try to recover the payment as a bounced check, pretending the debtor's request to cancel the check was mislaid, or even that it never happened. Then, the woman would be just another deadbeat claiming they weren't to blame for their returned check.

However, Stewart changed his mind and told me to submit the form to cancel the postdated check on file. Then, I should call the debtor back when the loan money was supposed to come through, and get payment. That would put the payment into next month.

"You don't want to start the month with a negative," he said. A check going NSF—insufficient funds—would come off my collection total. When the next sheet came out listing the department's success rate, my fee would appear as a negative number. I saw his point; starting the month in the hole, having to collect $1,100 just to get up to zero, would make it even more difficult to reach goal.

Even though my real goal is to learn about the business, not necessarily to succeed in it, I sometimes feel a keen desire to meet the expectations set before me. I find myself holding back from noncompliant things I would like to say—threats—hearing them slung all around me. "We'll garnish your paycheck; we'll put liens on your house," a woman across the aisle shouted into her phone one afternoon.

This was the same talk-off that Stew gave to my debtor previously, only in this case the threats were supposedly backed up and, therefore, allowed by law—at least, in our construction. It was a "prelegal" account, meaning the client who owned the debt would take the debtor to court as their next step. Or so we had been told by the client. Stew did not stop at threatening this woman with court, however. He quickly imagined that this course of action would result in a judgment against her, and garnishment of her wages.

"You're going to pay it either way," Stew said. "If you don't work something out with us, we'll take 25 percent of your paycheck, every week."But she dug in her heels, after having been fairly agreeable with me. I was ready to set her up for a down payment on a monthly plan when Stew got on, pushing for something by the end of the month. "Even $50, you're telling me you don't even have $50 you can pay on this bill that you've ignored for over a year?"Nope—it was a lot cheaper and easier to just hang up the phone. This was the closest I'd gotten to a payment in my new department, and I was angry that he blew it.

Action Item: Gather Supporting Evidence

If you wind up filing a complaint against a collector or taking them to court, you will need confirmation that their actions went over the line. Make notes of calls, including the time and date, and keep answering machine tapes of collectors' messages. It is often permissible to record calls from a collector; however, a minority of states are "two-party consent" states, in which it is necessary to tell a caller that you are taping. For more on this, see Chapter 24, "Preparing a Complaint."

18

NLE Means No Longer Employed

In the end, it wasn't only the way I was forced to treat debtors that drove me out of the collection business. There was also the corrosive effect that their hard luck stories were having on me.

Closeout fell on a Monday. Ann, the group manager above Stew, walked past the desks on her way out of a meeting. "C'mon people, only $250,000 to go," she quipped. I got nothing all day. Called my monthlies to try to sell them up into a settlement—no dice.

The entire office was short of goal. Managers gathered for hourly meetings to share their latest numbers. Then, suddenly, Ann was switched to a different department and we had a new group manager above Stew, a woman fairly new to the company who was transferred from another department. After announcing this, Stew added, with a straight face, "...and I will be leaving to manage a new office in Fort Lauderdale." Everyone just stared at him, too tense to recognize his joke or to laugh at it. "Uh, April fools," he said awkwardly. The new group leader has a deceptively mild voice that can gut you with one swipe. To an underperforming collector, I heard her say sweetly, "You need to step up and be a man, honey."

The board was looking anemic. Few payments in the green column, for cash today, and red postdates were for a paltry $50 or $100 each.

"You need to be getting more from your payers," our new manager said during her first day in our group, after humbly saying she'd be asking a lot of questions. Work the order of business. Pay in full.

Settle out. If they can only do monthly payments, push for 30 percent down.

"Boil it down to a few options for them," she advised. "It should be clear which option is the best choice." Why put a down payment on a full balance when you could settle the whole thing for a few hundred bucks? "Most people have $200 or $300 in immediate funds," she said. They might think of it as their rainy day stash or their cushion for a car repair bill or a doctor's visit for their kid. But to us, it's just sitting around in their bank account doing nothing. What a waste, when it could be performing a useful service—helping us meet our monthly goal and make bonus money.

Maybe most people do have a few hundred bucks lying around, but they were not eager to turn it over to me. The entire week redefined frustration. Instead of growing, my collection total was going backward. A postdate I had taken from a woman who worked in a bank came back as insufficient funds. She had stopped the check. It was the second NSF on her record, I saw after scrolling back through the account notes. A measly $100—why wouldn't she just pay her bill? She was working and didn't dispute the debt. The full balance was only $600. Maybe she knew she would never be taken to court over it, so she would never have to pay if she could just keep the dumb bill collectors fooled. By putting down that bogus postdated check, she won a whole month of freedom from collection calls.

Meanwhile, there is no word from Crystal, my formerly hot prospect in California. I skip-traced a bit and wound up speaking to her aunt at one of the phone numbers on the credit report. Crystal was on the move, the aunt said. It was difficult to keep up with her changing addresses. Could this itinerant deadbeat be the same Crystal who had seemed so genuine, bargaining to settle the bill?

I called the woman whose $1,100 payment had lifted me out of training, before it fell through. Supposedly, her home equity loan would provide money to pay off the debt. While listening to her phone ring, I opened her credit report. On closer inspection, the report didn't show any mortgage payments. I hadn't looked that far previously because she had come across with a check-by-phone immediately. Why probe a payer? Well, now I know why. Her story could be fictional, indicating that the payment was a fiction as well. It's possible the mortgage was entirely in her husband's name, or perhaps they owned their house outright, with no mortgage on record. Anyway, she didn't come to the phone.

I told Evan in the next booth my woes: three payments fallen through. I admitted to feeling a bit discouraged. "I'll get you a payment, buddy," Stew said, overhearing my talk with Evan. "It takes a while—tell him," he said to Evan, "you were here a year before you made goal." That must have been a nerve-racking year for Evan, assuming he needs an income.

I got the first "green" money, same-day payment since coming to the mixed purchase department, from a southern lady who sweetly agreed to give me a $100 down payment on an $800 debt, starting a monthly payment arrangement. She refused the settlement and wouldn't make further postdated checks for her future payments. "I'll call you each month; it won't be the same time each month," she said. "I'm going to be traveling soon."

"Oh, where are you going," I asked.

"Thailand."

"How exciting." While she scrounged in a desk drawer for her checkbook in order to read me the routing number, I imagined what one of the real collectors would make of her admission. "So, you're leaving an $800 debt hanging while you jet off to Thailand on vacation? How nice for you," they would say. "It won't bother you while you're there on the beach to think of how you've taken this money from your creditor? This creditor who advanced the money to you in good faith, expecting you to be an honorable person and repay your debt? They seem to have misjudged you." A hardball collector might have pried loose the settlement from her in one shot, or even payment in full. Then again, they might have blown the $100 that I did get. People react in different ways. Some knuckle under when a collector tries to shame them, but others get angry and dig in their heels. Anyway, I wasn't in the mood to pressure her. I needed a friendly voice at that point, one who was giving firm, same-day payment.

"Fred broke his cherry," Stew chanted in a singsong voice after I wrote the $100 on the board, trying to encourage me.

One light moment listening to an answering machine message broke up a long, futile afternoon. "If you're obsessive-compulsive, press one repeatedly...if you're codependent, have someone press 2 for you...if you're dyslexic, press six-nine, six-nine, six-nine..." Less funny are the messages people leave on their outgoing tape, hoping to screen out collection calls. These are folks who don't want to pay for the phone company's call-block service, which forces callers to state their name before the call is accepted. Instead, these people put an outgoing greeting on their answering machine, hoping to accomplish the same thing as the service. "This is me," said one of these greetings that exemplified the group. "If you're a friend or relative, leave a message. If you're selling something, hang up."

One woman's greeting said in a high, wavering voice, "If you're a bill collector, we don't have any money." This was sad and desperate, but ineffective. The message would increase calls, not reduce them. It confirmed that the phone number still belonged to the debtor. Most outgoing messages now reflect the obsolescence of trust. People leave the digital machine voice on their outgoing message. The robot voice does the screening, not even revealing who might live at the number. Recorded voice greetings are becoming rare. Of course, my experience might be skewed.

Toward the end of one night shift, I got a $9,000 account on the line, a personal loan. My talk-off was going well, I thought; the guy said he was looking into a second mortgage to pay off his outstanding debts. The intensity of the talk-off and the size of the account drew a little crowd behind my desk. People who had come over to chat with Evan stayed to watch me tussle for $9,000.

"Ask him for the name of the loan rep," whispered a veteran woman collector with flaming red hair. I handed her the headset, asking for a "second voice." This is the version of good-cop, bad-cop that collectors play. One will be the softy while another pretends to be the stern manager. The softy offers the settlement, and then the "manager" comes on and complains at the size of it, pretending to balk at this breach of company policy. Grudgingly, the "manager" says he or she will approve the outsize deal, but only if payment is made immediately, during the phone call. Then, the softy comes back on the line and acts apologetic about the manager's impolite behavior—and hopefully takes the grateful debtor's payment.

The red-haired woman to whom I handed my headset dealt with my debtor on a whole different level. "You must have income from somewhere," she told him. "You're telling me you survived on...$200 a week?" she said, dividing out the annual income figure that he had given me.

"I see you're reported as having $40,000 in income," she continued. I actually looked hard at the screen trying to see where she had found this gem of information, before I realized she'd made it up on the spot. Meanwhile she continued to prod his excuse of being tapped out.

"Don't get mad at me," she said into the phone. "The IRS supplies the figures; we're only the messenger." The IRS does no such thing. This was another total fabrication.

He already had a civil judgment on his credit record and all his accounts were in collections. He tried for sympathy, claiming to be a single parent who was struggling to keep food on his family's table, but the redhead was able to turn even this excuse around on him.

"Don't you put your children into this," she said, lowering her voice while putting more heat in it. "Children are a gift from God; they're not an excuse for you to hide behind."

"Wow," I murmured. She didn't get anything out of him, but neither did she let him create any moral wiggle room.

While I might not be collecting fee, at least my work experience is paying off in one way: I'm able to give advice to my indebted friends. During a long phone call, an old friend from my hometown admitted to having money problems of his own. His wife had racked up $13,000 in credit card debt. "There were three cards; well that's what I thought—now it turns out there's a fourth one," he told me.

He has been receiving reminder calls from the creditors about late payments, which is how he found out about the existence of the cards. He doesn't want to use the savings he has managed to squirrel away to pay off the debt. "Darlene's a wonderful person," he says repeatedly, but she is angry that he is meddling in financial affairs that she was trying to keep private.

That sends up a warning flare to me. Financial secrets are as damaging to a relationship as any other secret. I mail him two copies of forms that he can use to obtain his credit report, in the hope that he and his wife will review their reports together, fully sharing their financial lives. It's the second marriage for both of them. He has Social Security and a pension that's being steadily eroded by inflation. She still works part-time, but is pushing 60. Their house has shot up in value, but is poorly maintained. They'll have to borrow when the roof goes—but when are they going to have more income than now, to cover this additional spending?

One Friday morning as we drove in to work, I told Gary that I was done—finished. I'd had it. I planned to leave at lunch after picking up my check. I told him about my frustration, and how it was time I took care of some family business back home, requiring me to be out of town for a while.

"Oh man, I'm sorry to hear that. I'll miss you," he said.

"Well, I'll still be around to harass you," I told him. "I know where you live."

At lunch, we went to cash his check at my bank and he gave me the $45 he owed for gas and small loans. Having the afternoon off, he went to the bus stop to go home; I had decided to go back and finish out the day, having lost the nerve to simply walk out.

The relief I felt at quitting was mixed with regret. The question I had set out to answer remained murky. Can a debt collector abide by the rules and still bring in enough money to be successful? Not in my case. The $1,100 payment that lifted me out of training fell through after I made it to the floor. Strictly speaking, I fell far short of graduating. Even with the extra accounts, the "gifts" that had been slipped into my desk from management, I would have fallen about $500 short of the necessary $2,500 in fee. I was lucky to have worked on the floor at all, even for two weeks. Perhaps management bent the rules thinking my work habits would pay off eventually.

Yet my own failure as a lawful collector did not prove that it is impossible to succeed while obeying the rules. To everyone's surprise, my classmate Pamela graduated from training a few weeks early by hitting an enormous account. The balance was in the tens of thousands of dollars, and somehow the payment fell into her lap. She could be stern with debtors, but I can't imagine her slinging threats around. Raymond, another classmate I thought would wash out, pulled it together in the last few weeks of training to make it over the bar as well, quietly sitting at his desk and calling enough accounts to find the ripe ones.

Then again, being willing to use threats, lies, and intimidation was no handicap for the collectors who could pull it off. Bobby, the "fraud investigator," had been booted off the floor despite his aggressive threats, not because of them. It was his success with his implied threat of criminal action that won him a desk on the floor in the first place. Others with similar tactics continued to do well, like my classmate Trevor, who told me during the first week in Bart's classroom that he could "speak debtor," and like Barbara, with her convincing depiction of a paralegal getting ready to lower the boom. For all I know, they are still there, dialing away and reveling in their fat bonuses.

Just getting as far as I did came at a price. Even with my subpar performance, I had begun to develop the habitual distrust and suspicion that are attributes of a successful collector. Going back over the notes I made after work each day, I see a steady progression. My early concerns were about how to strictly comply with collection rules, and how to cope with heartwrenching hard-luck stories like the situation of Jim, Harley, and Bob, the little family that credit card debtor Samantha had left behind. As the days and weeks went by, these concerns gave way to thoughts of how to sharpen my talk-off and penetrate the deceptions of debtors, in order to put more money on the board.

It is clear how collectors can learn to inflict emotional abuse on debtors. It seems only fair when so much is heaped on them. After being taken in by the lies of deadbeats, it is easier to dismiss all hard-luck stories as dodges and exaggerations. If you don't, you risk being made a fool of—like me. I put my faith in easy lies, and then felt the sting of humiliation when everyone saw I was duped.

By five o'clock, most of my coworkers in the department have already gone home, having worked extra hours earlier in the week for closeout. As lax as the company is about debtor protection law, it adheres strictly to labor law. It is a serious infraction for a collector to work beyond 40 hours in a week, even by just a few minutes. I punch out and go back to my desk for the last time, put my aspirin and high-lighter into my pocket and pull my training certificate off the side of my cube, unplug my headset from the phone, and unhook the ID card from my belt.

"Good working with you," I say to Stew, who peers into his screen, reviewing the accounts we worked that day. I dangle my ID and headset. "Anything special I should do with these?"

"You done?" he says, looking away from his screen momentarily. I nod, oddly not trusting my voice. "I'll take care of those," he says. "You sure about this, buddy?"

"Yeah, it's not working out," I reply. "But I appreciate all your help." That seems to be all the explanation I have—and more than many people provide. It's more of a good-bye to the place than my training companion Ben gave or all the others who simply stopped showing up. So, I turn and make my way past the rows of cubicles, down the stairs, and out the door that I had entered for the first time on a frigid winter morning three months earlier.

I tried to leave with a little grace to reflect the gratitude I felt for the breaks that the agency had given me, not the least of which was hiring me in the first place. On my last call, I spent ten minutes with a debtor in Texas who seemed sincere about paying, but said he was out of work and had no money. I set up a return call for the following Monday, knowing that someone else would pick up and talk to the guy, if he called back as promised. A ringing phone does not go unanswered.

If I had not quit when I did after about three months, I might have seen more of the inside of collections. Probably not much more of it, though. My total was on track to fall far short of goal, and termination seemed likely, although my luck might have turned. Who knows, eventually I might have made it out of mixed purchase to one of the sought-after departments with fresher accounts. I might have sat near some of the members of the million-dollar club and learned their tricks. Just maybe, if I was there long enough, I would have become one of them.

My experience inside debt collection makes the industry's claims of rectitude appear to be part of an elaborate facade. At the agency where I worked, managers did not tell anyone, explicitly, to use forbidden tactics. They did not have to. The training in threats and lies was carried out by our coworkers, experienced mentors who passed along the tools of the trade. Managers merely looked the other way. As Mabel said about the unauthorized phone message that Joe had used, they don't want to see it. Even when the air was thick with threats and abuse, as during the monthly closeout push, the message from management was to push harder still. The compliance department, whose supposed mission was to enforce collection rules, was at best ineffective, at worst a sham. Collectors knew when they were being recorded, invalidating the compliance department's supposedly secret auditing of their calls. From what I saw, compliance handed out a rare slap on the wrist while it recorded what must have been faultless collection calls because collectors knew when they were being recorded. The company could present an image of strict probity to outsiders, while in reality it rewarded shakedown practices.

This went on at a collection agency that stands solidly in the mainstream of the industry. As Bart told us on the first day, the company is long established, not a recent upstart, and it counted several large credit card issuers among its clients. I do not doubt that the outlaw collection tactics that I saw pale in comparison to what goes on at even less-scrupulous firms. Some of the very largest agencies have a worse regulatory record, such as the pattern of abuses charged at industry leader NCO Group. Then there are other operations modeled on the likes of CAMCO and Lenahan, where the harshest threats were standard practice.

A key fact about the industry today is that the Lenahans and CAMCOs are competing in the same arena as the more legitimate agencies. This is because the wide-open debt market, where accounts are bought and sold, distributes accounts wherever the returns are the highest. At my employer, a significant fraction of clients were debt buyers. These are faceless investment firms that no one outside the industry has heard of. These businesses are only interested in the return on their investment. Unlike direct creditors, such as the banks that issue credit cards, they have no image to protect. They can send, or sell, their accounts to boiler room scam artists as easily as to more legitimate agencies. This gives the mainstream collection industry a stark choice: Match the scammers threat for threat, lie for lie, or risk being pushed out of business by them. After all, Congress found it necessary to outlaw threats and lies back in 1977 for a reason: They work. Yes, some debtors respond to a settlement offer or a long-term payment plan, but many do not. For them, threats of lawsuits, wage garnishment, or even prison might be the only collection tactics that get the bill paid.

Another thing I learned was how an entire industry of workers could be trained to leave their feelings of compassion behind when they came to work. Certainly, the financial incentives—the lucrative bonus for success, combined with the specter of job loss as a consequence of failure—were part of the reason. The bonus assembly, where monthly bonus checks of more than $10,000 each were handed out to the best collectors, made a strong impression on me and my fellow trainees. So did the sight of the empty seats left by coworkers who had washed out.

However, the financial pressures and rewards were only part of the explanation. Who was it that trained collectors to be hard, to shed their sympathy? Debtors, that's who. As trainees, we worked accounts that were usually years-old and well "beaten down." Many other collectors before me had already done their best to squeeze cash out of them. These accounts were the bottom of the barrel, the hard-core nonpayers. Pity the innocent debtor, or the person claiming not to be a debtor, who is up against a collector trained on these hard cases. Among this group, consumers who truthfully say they do not owe money are a rarity. Unless they can back up their story, it will be dismissed. In fact, their excuses are likely to ignite a collector's anger and set off his more aggressive impulses.

Hardened by debtors' ruses and under pressure to meet goal, collectors view the accounts provided to them as solid obligations, not rife with inaccuracies and loaded with extra fees. Anyone who answers the phone linked to the account seems like a deadbeat until proven otherwise. You say you don't owe the money? They all say that. You're not the debtor? Prove it. Or put him on the phone.

Only a few of the collectors that I met actually seemed to enjoy issuing harsh threats to strangers, like my pod mate Joe. Most of them simply adapted to their jobs the way most people are required to do. Like an athlete putting on a game face, they repeated the industry's code, that there is a moral imperative to pay one's bills. In this respect, the collectors I know are like the salespeople who tell themselves that they are helping people by introducing them to a fantastic product or the defense attorneys who get criminals off the hook and tell themselves they are fulfilling a vital role in a justice system, by ensuring due process for the accused. We are all just doing our jobs in the larger scheme of things, even the guards of the new debtors' prison.

The incentive I did not expect to find was the powerful desire to do well in the eyes of one's peers. You might not imagine that debt collectors would be all that sensitive to the opinions of others. Indeed, it is true that they let criticism from outsiders slide off them easily. Among our own, however, it is a different story. Whether you call it peer pressure or professional pride, the drive to equal your coworkers and earn their respect is a strong one. That is as true in collections as anywhere else—maybe even more so. Every morning, the whiteboard is wiped clean of yesterday's red, green, and blue ink, and stands ready to display what you can do.

Action Item: Avoid High-Cost Credit Counselors

If you need help negotiating with debt collectors, you might want to seek help from a credit-counseling agency. However, there are a broad range of companies offering credit-counseling services, and their costs and abilities vary widely. Even nonprofit debt counseling services might not necessarily be low cost. You can obtain referrals to accredited counseling services through the National Foundation for Credit Counseling, whose Web address is www.nfcc.org. To learn how to negotiate with creditors yourself and avoid counseling fees, see Chapter 25, "Negotiating a Debt Settlement."

19

Solutions

In the time since I worked in collections, a sweeping overhaul of credit card practices has taken place. The Credit Card Accountability, Responsibility, and Disclosure Act—or Credit CARD Act, for short—was signed in the spring of 2009, with its main provisions taking effect the following year. Among the law's several provisions, two will do the most to reduce costs for consumers. The act limits the imposition of overlimit fees, and it forbids retroactive interest-rate hikes on a balance in good standing. Credit card companies still deserve to turn a profit, President Barack Obama said at the signing ceremony. "We just want to make sure that they do so while upholding basic standards of fairness, transparency, and accountability."[1]

Those basic standards of fairness were not in place when the nation's credit card debt was being piled up. Penalty interest and fees that have already been added to account balances are unaffected by the legislative overhaul. That existing debt will be paid down with the help of debt collectors—at least the portion of it that goes delinquent. Despite calls from regulators as well as consumer advocates to fix collection laws now that credit card practices have been addressed, there is no companion to the CARD Act for the collection industry.

However, changes that will help consumers in their battle with unfair and harassing collection tactics might be in the works, after decades of inaction. In 2009, the Federal Trade Commission, the chief agency charged with enforcing debtor protection law, admitted problems. More than a year after it held a workshop discussion to examine the law, it published a report calling for reform.[2] Among other things, the reform proposals include requiring creditors to disclose a breakdown of the debt by principal, interest, and fees in their validation notice. This would provide useful negotiating information to debtors hit with exorbitant fees. In addition, debt collectors would be required to conduct "reasonable" investigations of a disputed debt, instead of just dumping it back into the queue. Collectors would also be prohibited from calling people on their mobile phones without their consent.

The industry association got behind some proposals for reform that came out of the workshop. Specifically, ACA International supports restrictions on the sale and resale of disputed debts.[3] Creditors as well as debt buyers should have to verify a disputed debt before reselling it. The industry also seeks a requirement that would work hand in hand with this, wherein financial institutions would be required to keep on file the data backing the debts they sell. Information on the debtors' identities and locations should be available to the buyer of the debts, the industry said. Although these requirements seem designed to help collectors bring in money, they should also head off some of the abuses connected with debt resale, when disputed debts are simply passed along to another collector, perpetuating an endless cycle of harassment for an innocent consumer.

Finally, the FTC urged an increase in the $1,000 statutory penalty for collection violations. To deter infractions, the amount should be increased to reflect inflation since it was adopted back in 1977, and should be updated periodically in the future, the report recommended. The agency does not specify in its statement the amount of the increase, but the Consumer Price Index has more than tripled since 1977.[4] The corresponding increase in the statutory penalty would bring it to about $3,500 today.

The penalty is particularly important because it constitutes the main deterrent to illegal threats and lies. When it comes to debt collection, the job of consumer protection falls mainly on consumers themselves. The Fair Debt Collection Practices Act spells out the rules collectors are supposed to live by, but it has never envisioned the Federal Trade Commission, or any other agency, would be able to oversee every collection agency to ensure the rules are followed. Instead, the law sets out consumers' private right of action in order that they may police the industry while protecting themselves from unfair practices.

Some in Washington have taken up the call to update consumer protection law. Senator Carl Levin, a Democrat from Michigan, recommended that debtor protections be rolled into the duties of a proposed new consumer financial protection agency, which is one of the elements of a sweeping financial reform plan. As 2009 drew to a close, Levin released a Government Accountability Office report that backed his call for tighter debt collection regulation. It trumpeted many of the points that consumer advocates have been making for years—complaints against collectors are surging, constituting the number-one complaint received by many state regulators as well as the FTC, while government crackdowns in any given year are sparse. Federal agencies took only 32 formal enforcement actions against abusive debt collectors during the past 10 years, while thousands of complaints rolled in.[5]

"The volume of complaints and general lack of enforcement show that abusive debt collection practices are a big and growing problem for many Americans," Levin said in releasing the report.[6]

Some states that have enacted tough regulation of the collection industry point the way to drastic reductions in shakedown practices. If their protections were extended across the nation, collection scammers would find it difficult to operate for long. Maine requires collectors to post bond so that scammers cannot hit and run, ducking the consequences of their actions by shutting their doors or filing for bankruptcy. Maine joins Minnesota and some other states in requiring licensing for collection companies. If a national licensing system were in place, scammers who ignore the rules should be easy to identify and shut down. Regulators and individual debtors would be able to check licensing data to see if calls originate from a legitimate collector. Furthermore, with licensed collectors required to post bond, in effect a prepayment of fines, they would have a powerful incentive to abide by the rules.

However, under the FDCPA, it is still up to consumers to protect themselves from collection scams and shakedowns. The advice "buyer beware" applies to debtors as well as consumers. As with buying a car or signing a loan, knowing your rights is the key to getting a fair deal. The following pages provide an overview of collection processes in a how-to format for debtors—or nondebtors who are harassed by collection calls—to guard against collection threats, lies, and intimidation. The collection process is explored from identifying a collector, validating a debt, disputing a collection attempt, collecting evidence of unlawful practices, and preparing to bring a case under collection law. Also examined is the role that credit reports play in the process, and tips for achieving a debt settlement that can cut the amount due by hundreds of dollars.

Part 2

Coping with Collections

20

Stopping Collection Calls

Among the most common calls that collectors make are the ones that reach the wrong people. The industry makes roughly one billion "consumer contacts" per year, according to a Federal Reserve study based on industry-provided data.[1] Many of the calls go to people who happen to share a last name with a debtor, live at their old address, or—most frustrating for the consumer—have inherited a debtor's old phone number.

These wrong numbers should be the easiest collection attempts to deflect. Common sense would seem to dictate that collectors who have reached the wrong person would quickly drop their efforts. Why would they waste their time dunning someone who doesn't owe money? Unfortunately, it's not that simple. Because so many actual debtors make the same claim, collectors are highly suspicious of people who say they have nothing to do with the debt. As irritating as that is for the innocent nondebtor, it might not be so easy to halt the calls.

What is more, the persistence of phone and address records in commercial databases and the credit reporting system can make the calls a recurring problem—for some people, a recurring nightmare—as a succession of different collectors, and even different collection agencies, retrieve the same information again and again. Collectors are trained to call all the numbers associated with the account, even ones that are years old, in hopes of finding a relative or acquaintance who can provide new contact information.

Here are some tactics for putting an end to these calls:

- **Don't overreact.** The natural response is to be irritated and even angry. That won't help with a collector. They're used to people getting mad and demanding to speak to their manager. You won't succeed in getting them in trouble for trying to verify your identity, even though it is unfair that they're calling you out of the blue with something that's not your problem. You have a right to be angry, but holding your temper will result in a better outcome.

- **Provide minimal identifying information.** It is not your obligation to prove that you aren't the debtor. You also do not have to deny knowing or being related to the debtor, whether they're a neighbor, a relative, or a complete stranger.

- **Turn the tables.** If they persist in demanding identifying details from you to prove that you aren't the person they seek, say calmly that you've already told them they have the wrong party, and ask that they put your number on the agency's "do not dial" list. Say that any further calls will constitute harassment under the Fair Debt Collection Practices Act. Inform them that you will record further calls to protect yourself from harassment; then do it. If the calls continue and you document them, you should be able to interest a consumer lawyer in bringing a complaint against the firm.

I have been on both sides of this kind of call. The message on my voice mail was from a robot voice urging me to call an 800 number during regular business hours. I called back and told a woman, who answered at some collection bureau, my name.

"Not Frederick Williams?" she asked.

"Nope."

"You've never been Frederick Williams?"

"No, I think you have the wrong person."

"Are you sure?"

At this point, I'm starting to get steamed, but she dropped her line of questioning and said she'd remove my number from her list.

As run-ins with the collection industry go, this one went exceptionally smoothly, without threats or even harsh language. Still, it leaves some questions.

How did my phone number—my cell phone number—get on her "list" in the first place? Having been in her place, I can answer that. She probably ran a directory search for her debtor, and my name and location were close enough to give it a shot.

Furthermore, the woman's call followed earlier ones from an automated system, which should have stopped the collection attempt. The robot voice said it was trying to reach Frederick Williams, and if that wasn't me, to press a certain number. I pressed the number. I might as well have tried to engage the machine voice in a discussion about rights to privacy. The instruction to press the number was probably some sort of placebo to placate the innocent, wrongly called consumer because the calls seeking Frederick Williams kept on coming. Until, that is, I called back and satisfied a collector that I really wasn't the supposed debtor whom she was trying to reach.

A woman in California, a doctor who inherited a debtor's old phone number, had a less cordial run-in with a collector calling from a supposed law office in Buffalo. She received an infuriating series of phone calls, some of them early in the morning. The collectors were looking for a woman named Blair. The doctor was familiar with the name because she had previously received calls for someone named Blair. The doctor assumed Blair must be the name of the family who previously had her phone number. However, when she explained this to the collectors, they didn't drop their attempt. To the contrary, they demanded that the doctor give them her correct name and address, plus her birth date and other identifying information, supposedly to show that she wasn't the person they were seeking.

Most frustrating to the doctor was that she was unable to prove she wasn't some deadbeat who was trying to weasel out of an obligation, at least not without turning over all kinds of personal information that she definitely did not want the collectors to have. She was reluctant to file a complaint with the Better Business Bureau or state consumer protection authorities for other reasons.

"The people who file such complaints often are deadbeats who are trying to escape their obligations by attacking the creditor," she wrote to me in an e-mail. She felt that she wouldn't be taken seriously. "But I was an innocent bystander, with no ulterior motive. Even when talking to a wrong number, these people behaved like criminals."

Out of curiosity, she checked old phone records to see if she could find this Blair that was the source of so much irritation. Although her number had been previously assigned to someone I will call Blair, it was not the Elizabeth Blair that the collectors were seeking. They had found a last name that matched their debtor, in the area they were looking for, and called the number thinking it might be a relative. Who knows, Elizabeth might even be living with this relative now. If someone—anyone—answers the phone, the collector's instinct is to doggedly keep demanding to speak to the debtor.

Providing a minimal amount of identifying information, such as the last two digits of your SSN or your last name, should be enough to end the calls. Unless you have just moved or recently obtained the number, the lookup databases that collectors use will confirm that you are someone other than the debtor they are looking for. If not, you'll want to refer to subsequent pages on how to identify the agency where the calls are coming from, to begin the process of making a complaint and potentially bringing the agency to court for harassment.

21

Checking Out a Collector

All the rules of fair play spelled out in the Fair Debt Collection Practices Act assume one important thing: To hold the collector and his agency accountable, you have to know the identity of the company with which you are dealing. However, that isn't always the case. Misrepresentation, after all, is one of the most common complaints that consumers make about collectors.

At my office, the official training course taught us to identify our company by its correct name to the debtor (and the debtor only, unless asked), but individual collectors interpreted this with a great deal of latitude. Some of my coworkers told people that they were calling "from Visa" or "on behalf of Bank of America," or whatever other creditor originated the account. Their plan was to get the debtor to agree to pay the bill first, before getting into the messy details of just who was demanding the payment. Other coworkers went beyond that and claimed to be investigating fraudulent use of a credit card and other ploys—tricks that weren't covered during our training, but were nevertheless tolerated.

Some collection agencies have chosen names that happen to sound like the name of a law firm, such as "O'Connor & Green," to make up an example based on a real firm. Other collectors, rather than implying that they are calling from a law firm, will make that claim outright. In addition, there are also rent-a-lawyer offices that are really just call centers that have adopted the name of a lawyer to strike fear into debtors' hearts with threats of seized property and garnished wages.

The chances of facing actual court action from one of these rent-a-lawyer outfits is slim to none, so it is important to distinguish them from collection law operations that do use the court process.

Even mainstream agencies can be cagey about their information. Collectors at my company rarely disclosed the mailing address because we were coached only to take verified forms of payment like check-by-phone or wire funds. To us, an offer to send a paper check via regular mail was the same as a refusal to pay, so little faith did we have in the debtor following through.

Although collectors might not be forthcoming about where they work, there's one piece of identifying information that they can rarely avoid disclosing: a phone number. Either coming through your Caller ID, if not blocked, or left as a message in order for you to call back, a working phone number is usually something the collector must part with, if they hope to receive a call back and have any hope of collecting a payment. Reverse lookup directories can yield the name of the agency. Even simply typing the number into a search window on Google or Yahoo! might yield the agency name, along with the comments of other consumers about their dealings with the company.

Once you are armed with the name of the company, further background can be found in official records. The State of Maine Department of Professional & Financial Regulation, Consumer Credit Protection Bureau maintains a searchable list of agencies licensed to do business in the state. Minnesota's Department of Commerce also licenses collectors that do business in that state, and consumers can search for license status of both businesses and individual collectors. Nevada's Department of Business and Industry, Division of Financial Institutions also lists licensed agencies. Although these agencies exist to protect residents of their states against unfair collections, the information these states maintain is available, and useful, to out-of-state consumers. The Better Business Bureau might also be helpful in finding information, at least on larger companies. In my test of a dozen agencies, the BBB national Web site was able to give an address for the largest collectors.

According to the FTC, collectors who transmit a false phone number through the Caller ID system are in violation of the misrepresentation clause of the FDCPA.[1] Whether collectors should be required to transmit their number through Caller ID at all, rather than block it, has not been determined, according to the FTC, leaving collectors free to block their number.[2] However, most collection agencies, even those using harsh shakedown tactics, disclosed their real phone number at some point. Most collection calls reach an answering machine, after all; and those calls are wasted if the collector doesn't leave a way for you to call them back.

Regulators also use phone numbers as an identifier. The Federal Trade Commission's database contains a column for the phone number of the caller, so it can track complaints on that basis, even when consumers aren't sure of the company that called them. It is possible to make a complaint about a collection call with only the number as an identifier. The agency can probably link the number to the source of the call.

22

Using Collection Law

The U.S. Fair Debt Collection Practices Act prohibits collectors from harassing, threatening, and lying to their targets. It also says that collectors must stop calling if a consumer simply asks them to do so, in writing. They are also supposed to provide verification of a debt in response to a written request.

Of course, if collectors and collection agencies obeyed the law and consistently played by those rules, there would not be tens of thousands of complaints about them pouring into the regulatory offices each year. Hundreds of consumer lawyers who chiefly represent debtors would have to find another specialty, or another line of work. There would be no need for this book. Unfortunately, collectors cannot be counted on to play by the rules, as I learned firsthand. Collectors might learn the rules mainly to know how to skirt them. However, because the Fair Debt Collection Practices Act establishes your rights in the collection process, knowing its key provisions is an essential starting point on the way to getting a fair shake. Knowing its terms and procedures, and using them during the collection process, will strengthen your grounds for a lawsuit if the collector's tactics warrant going that route. In addition, showing awareness of the law by using its terminology in discussions with collectors will demonstrate to them that you are aware of your rights and their responsibilities, which should make them think twice about using unfair and illegal tactics.

Here then is a quick rundown of the major protections and remedies that the FDCPA affords consumers.

Collectors cannot:

- Use false threats or falsely imply that they work for an attorney or that a legal action will be filed against you. (Figuring out whether a threat is false is the subject of Chapter 21, "Checking Out a Collector.")
- Call you at inconvenient times, such as before 8:00 a.m. or after 9:00 p.m. Nor may they call you at work after you inform them that it is not allowed.
- Use obscene language or call repeatedly as an annoyance tactic to harass.
- Discuss your debt with third parties, such as relatives or neighbors. However, they may talk to these third parties to locate you.
- Misstate the amount owed or tack on additional fees such as "collection charges." However, there can be exceptions to that if the contract governing the debt allows such fees.

Collectors must:

- Provide a "validation notice" on first contact or within five days after first calling you. This should contain the name of the creditor, the amount owed, and the process for disputing the bill.
- Cease contacting you after receiving a "cease communication" letter from you. Make sure to send this certified with a receipt as proof. The collector may respond to acknowledge receipt or to inform you what steps the creditor will take next. Communication of a legal process is not covered by the cease communication letter.
- Provide you with verification of a debt upon your written request—again, be sure to send this by certified mail and keep the receipt. The request must be made within 30 days of being contacted by the collector. Just what qualifies as verification is open to some interpretation. Collectors say they're not required to send you detailed copies of the creditor's original bill. They will likely send a summary statement of the total that

the creditor claims is due. On a credit card bill, for example, this summary would not necessarily include a breakout of fees and interest charges, or a detail of the dates that the debt was incurred, the individual charges, or the merchants involved. From many collectors, verification consists of little more than the information contained in the validation letter, a bald statement of what you supposedly owe and the name of the creditor. That's probably the only information that the collector has.

Actions that would "harass and oppress" are forbidden, as is "abuse" of the consumer. This has been interpreted as frequent phone calling and shouting. What constitutes a violation is subjective, but the terminology is important. If you tell a collector that you feel that his or her conduct is harassing or abusive, you have put them on notice. They might disagree; typically, my coworkers would react by saying that, on the contrary, they were trying to impart critical information about the status of a debt that the consumer needed to know. However, having put the collector on notice using the terminology in the law will strengthen your case against them later, if the harassment continues.

Calls at work are a particular problem, and collectors know it. Under the law, you should be able to stop calls at work by saying they are not convenient, and that your employer disapproves of them or doesn't allow them. Some states offer higher standards of protection from this tactic. But collectors eagerly call you at work because they know it exerts pressure—especially if your end of the call can be overheard by coworkers. In addition, of course, being reached at a workplace means the debtor cannot claim to be without income to pay the debt. The collector will usually bargain with you when asked to stop calling at work. "Well then," he or she might say, "let's set a time to talk on your home phone. Or better yet, let's get this resolved now so I don't have to call you at work again." The law is on your side here, however, so you don't have to bargain to make these calls stop.

Once a collector has your workplace number, however, the temptation is great to use it as leverage. One starkly illegal tactic is to fax wage garnishment papers or other such documents to a general fax number at the consumer's office. Another ploy is to use an automated switchboard to reach your coworkers. Some companies provide the names and extension numbers of employees on an automated system. All the collector has to do is keep working through the list of employees to collect every name and extension available on the system. In one case that came to the attention of the Maine consumer protection bureau's office, a rogue collector issued threats of a lawsuit to one of the debtor's coworkers who happened to share his last name. The coworker told her friends about the strange call, and the story got around the office, to the embarrassment of the debtor.[1]

Cell phone calls are another particular problem, and have received regulatory attention lately. Because they cost the recipient money, cell phone calls represent a special case. In January 2008, the collection industry won an exemption from the Telephone Consumer Protection Act allowing auto-dialers to be used to contact debtors on their cell phones. The Federal Communications Commission ruled that, by giving his or her cell number to a creditor, a consumer gave consent to be called in regard to the debt using that number. However, this ruling has been the subject of court action and was briefly struck down in a California case where the judgment was later vacated. The FTC, in its proposals for revision to the FDCPA, seeks new treatment for cell phone calls, as they weren't anticipated by the original act in 1977.[2] There might be more protections coming on this score, as the FTC recommendations state that the cost of receiving a cell phone call to the debtor needs to be addressed. "Consumers should not have to pay to be contacted by a debt collector," the agency's February 2009 report on changes to the FDCPA states.

Moreover, the mobility of cell phones means that collectors cannot know for certain the time zone where a consumer is located, making it difficult to comply with provisions that prohibit calls before 8:00 a.m. or after 9:00 p.m. At the agency where I worked, the phone system blocked calls to certain area codes based on the time of day in that time zone. With cell phones, of course, there's no guarantee that the owner of the phone is in the time zone associated with the phone's area code.

Collectors do not spend a lot of time worrying about these details. They expect that the phone number on the account was provided by the debtor when they borrowed money. The creditor, after all, wasn't just going to hand over money without getting a valid telephone number where the borrower could be reached. Therefore, collectors feel entitled to call that number as long as the bill remains unpaid. If it is a cell phone, or if the debtor has traveled to a different time zone in which it might be too early or late for a debt collection call, this is a secondary issue outside the collector's control.

This kind of thinking on the part of collectors can give you grounds for argument in protesting the collectors' actions, both in complaints to the company and later in a legal challenge under the FDCPA, if that route is the one taken. If you can show in court that a collector violated any part of the law, the collector is obligated to pay you a fine of up to $1,000, an amount that might be raised substantially under the proposals being considered in Congress. In addition, the court will set "reasonable" attorney's fees. Usually, consumer lawyers take these cases on a contingency-fee basis, relieving you of responsibility for their fees.

From my experience, these provisions of the FDCPA were the most useful to know in confrontations with collectors, but this is not meant as a complete treatment of the ins and outs of the FDCPA. For more information, the Federal Trade Commission provides an overview on its Web site, at www.ftc.gov. The state attorney general or consumer protection office in your state might have useful materials as well. Some states' debtor protection laws add measures that go beyond the protections afforded by the FDCPA.

23

Reading Your Credit Reports

Knowing what appears on your credit report—and what does not—is essential for anyone preparing to negotiate a debt settlement. What your report reveals will give the collector a picture of your ability to pay, forming the basis for negotiation.

Thanks to provisions of the Fair Credit Reporting Act, it is easy to see exactly what your report says. Consumers can obtain a free copy of their report from each of the three reporting bureaus once a year. However, despite all the attention that has recently been paid to the credit report, and advertising on television and elsewhere that urges everyone to examine their credit history, there remain some misconceptions about these records:

- **Information disappears from your credit report after seven years.** It is true that most negative account information should melt off your credit report after seven years, except for some court and tax lien entries. But other information can remain on the report indefinitely. Old addresses, phone numbers, and employers, as well as open but inactive accounts, can remain on your report. This subjects your past to greater scrutiny and provides a debt collector with useful information that goes beyond mere identifying details that the addresses and employers are supposed to provide.

- **Delinquent debts are erased after they've been paid.** Not only do these demerits remain on your report for seven years, but the fact that they have been paid might not even be noted. It is up to you to make sure that the creditor or the collector who received your payment files that information with the credit bureau to update your report. If it is not, you can push to have the report corrected by using the dispute procedures available under the Fair Credit Reporting Act.

- **Credit reports are for granting credit.**   True as far as it goes, but under a provision of the relevant consumer protection law, other uses are permissible. Insurers, employers, landlords, and other "valid" business users are allowed to view your report, a broadly defined group that includes debt collectors.

Many people new to the collection process are alarmed that collectors have such extensive information about them. The profile of your account status and history, plus supplementary information including past addresses, employers, and identifying details, such as your middle initial and Social Security number, make the report a trove of useful information. Charge accounts, credit cards, car loans, and mortgages should all be on the report, as well as "public record" information, usually court judgments, tax liens, and bankruptcy filings. Bank fees and bounced checks to merchants are not necessarily included, but may appear as well.

The reports show when accounts were opened, the credit limit, payment history, and account status—whether in good status, closed, delinquent, or charged-off. Sometimes bills from other collectors and debt consolidators will show up among the accounts, including collectors that specialize in medical collections. This inadvertently supplies additional information about you and your situation. Credit reports aren't supposed to disclose medical problems, but collectors can often spot a pattern of significant medical debts based on the creditors and collectors listed on the report. Finally, there's a record of the companies that have requested your credit report recently, other than for unsolicited credit card offers termed "promotional" inquiries.

In the upside-down world of collections, this information gets an unusual spin. Although demerits on your report hurt you at the loan office, they help you when dealing with a debt collector. The worse your credit situation looks, the less likely you are to pay, and the less time and effort a collector will invest in you. Conversely, the more resources you appear to have, by virtue of having paid-up accounts, the harder the collector will pursue you, and the more difficult it will be to negotiate a settlement.

What can help you on your credit report? Mainly, things that are not on it. Expenses and problems that the collector is not aware of make a difference in your ability to pay, and can help you win a bigger settlement in negotiations to reduce a debt. Job loss, for example, might have occurred and left you with limited resources. Your current employment status is not reflected on the credit report. Court action against you, even the beginning of foreclosure on your house, will not appear on your report until official documents are filed, and there might be a time lag even then before the legal action is reported to the credit bureaus. Similarly, a bankruptcy won't appear until after the papers are filed. In addition, records for charge accounts or merchant bills will lack the most recent month of your payment history.

Moreover, the collector might not have the most recent copy of your report on file. To save costs, the collection agency where I worked prevented us from ordering a new report if one had been ordered within the past 60 days. So, it is likely that your most recent credit history, within at least the past two or three months, is a blank to the collector.

Marital status, which is dealt with only peripherally on your report, can be a major influence on your finances and your ability to pay. The report may name your spouse, usually as "spouse or coapplicant," based on joint accounts you have together; and that notation may remain on accounts that remain on your report even after the marriage is dissolved. A collector may infer that a divorce has occurred by the closing of joint accounts and the opening of single accounts—especially if this is accompanied by the discharge of a mortgage, indicating the possible sale of the marital home. However, these signals aren't always present, especially for couples and unmarried cohabitants who keep their finances separate. Yet even for them, the financial impact of splitting up, with its consequences of lower pooled income and higher, unshared expenses, are just as troublesome as they are for couples who share every account.

Credit reports are also haphazard when it comes to your work history. Your employers will only be reported to the extent that you had to reveal them to creditors, landlords, or merchants as part of a credit application. Because employers are technically on the report only as an extra form of identification, there is no effort to make the list comprehensive or up to date.

Collectors are very interested in your employment status and history. Usually, the account they are collecting will have a "POE," place of employment, that was reported as part of the credit application. If that employer is out of date, however, they will frequently try to determine your current employer. Checking the credit report might yield more recent information—or more places to call in an effort to pry information from your former coworkers.

Preparing for negotiation is one good reason why it is essential to know what your credit reports say about you. The other very good reason is that your reports may contain incorrect and out-of-date information. According to a study by the U.S. Public Interest Research Group, 79 percent of credit reports contain some sort of error, and more than half contained incorrect or out-of-date identifying information.[1] Furthermore, reports from the three major bureaus, Experian, TransUnion, and Equifax, may contain different account information as well. The data available to them is not necessarily reported to all three bureaus because it is furnished by individual creditors. Thus, it is important to check all three credit reports. If a collector claims not to see an entry on your credit report, ask which bureau he obtained it from. Having all three reports to the collector's one conveys an advantage to you in negotiation.

One thing that debtors don't need to worry about is their credit score. Although this single number is, perhaps, very important in the credit-granting world, it isn't much use to collectors. They are more interested in whether you have open accounts in good standing, recent applications for further credit, and current employment.

It should not be necessary to describe how to go about obtaining your credit report. All consumers are legally entitled to a free copy of each bureau's report every 12 months. However, the reporting agencies have found a way to turn this requirement into a revenue-generating opportunity by up-selling people into fee-based services. To get the actual free report online, use the Federal Trade Commission-approved site at www.annualcreditreport.com. Even here, it will be necessary to avoid offers for things like credit-watch services and FICO score numbers, once you are linked through the portal to the reporting bureaus' systems. Also, it is a good idea to stock up on printer paper beforehand because the formatting of the sites does not make it easy to save a copy of the report electronically—at least not one that will display properly after saving it to your computer.

At a business like a collection office, users of your report will have the advantage of looking at your data any way they choose because they will have it loaded digitally and can query the report to display selected data. So, when discussing your credit history with a collector, be aware that they will have the information in a different format than the one you see, even if both reports are from the same credit bureau.

24

Preparing a Complaint

Enforcement of the Fair Debt Collection Practices Act is mainly left up to debtors themselves. The law provides a private right of action, empowering debtors or "alleged debtors" to bring justice against abusive collectors, usually with the help of an attorney who specializes in consumer law. If the debtor's case prevails, the court will direct the collector to pay court costs and the debtor's "reasonable" attorney fees, as determined by the court. The collector will also pay the debtor a statutory penalty of up to $1,000, a fine that the FTC has proposed be tripled. Finally, the act provides that consumers be awarded their actual damages. Lawyers who handle these cases tell me that damages can be worth far more than the statutory award, but are more difficult to prove than a violation of the act. Damages like lost wages or medical bills that stem from unfair or abusive collection actions can carry a high price tag; however, proving such damages is far from an open-and-shut case.

You will need an attorney if you decide to sue. That attorney will determine the best way to conduct your case from a legal perspective, which is not within the coverage of this book. However, before you try to interest a lawyer in your case, it helps to have done some work of your own. Before taking a case, consumer attorneys will weigh the likelihood of winning the action. You can improve your odds greatly with preparation to substantiate your claim. A collector's first response to a complaint is usually to deny the debtor's version of events and portray the debtor as a deadbeat who is trying to squirm out of paying. Their own records, such as collectors' call notes, will likely show no indication that the collector acted improperly. So, it will be up to you to recognize violations and to document or substantiate them, to rebut the collector's denials. Showing up at a lawyer's office with only your recollection of a collector's harassing or misleading conduct won't get you to court, no matter how great your sense of outrage.

So, how do you substantiate claims of a collector's misconduct? The way to back up your story is with your own notes, recordings of telephone calls, and the statements of third parties, such as family members, neighbors, housemates, or coworkers who received calls and spoke to collectors. Noting the date and time of calls and the number from a caller ID device helps substantiate your version of events.

As the head of Maine's state consumer protection agency once told me, "Nothing beats a tape."[1] There are legal complications involved in secret taping, but secrecy shouldn't be necessary. First, the recordings left on an answering machine are fair game, and might be a smoking gun of collection abuses. In researching court and regulatory cases, it is surprising how often collectors leave blatantly illegal messages on an answering machine, knowing their words are being recorded. In a message left for one Idaho consumer, a collector identified himself as a "fraud investigator" and said that he had enough "evidence" of the consumer's supposed wrongdoing to file criminal charges of fraud, based on the consumer's unpaid credit card balance. Then he tacked on a charge of grand larceny, supposedly because the balance due on the card was over $1,000. "I do have the authority to make this a criminal case," he said, adding that he would do so unless the debtor called him back that day.

Of course, being unable to pay off a charge account that you opened in good faith is not fraud. Nor are debt collectors empowered to bring criminal charges against you—or civil charges, for that matter. Court action is the province of an attorney. Real prosecutors won't call you and warn you of pending charges, then offer to drop the case in return for payment.

The brief message on the answering machine provided evidence of the collector's misrepresentation and threatening behavior. Such brazen and intentional violations of the FDCPA make a case against the collector a slam dunk. The regulator who had obtained the tape used it in a case that prohibited the collection company from calling Idaho consumers.[2]

Recording a call is permissible in all states if you notify the caller that you are taping. If the collector later disputes having been given this warning, it will go under the heading of their word against yours. What will not be in dispute is what was said; and, if the content of the tape reveals false representations and harassment, it will indicate that the collector's word cannot be taken at face value.

Most attorneys and regulatory officials seem to agree that the best recording for court purposes is an actual, physical tape, from a cassette or microcassette recorder of the sort that is rapidly being made obsolete by digital recording technology. Despite the advantages of digital recording, the new technology isn't the best for legal purposes, consumer attorneys say. A digital audio file may be edited more easily than a physical tape, or so most courts understand. Tape recording technology is familiar to courts, and most are aware of the existence of techniques that can detect manipulation of an audiotape if its contents are called into question.

Dispassionate third parties might also be able to provide independent corroboration of a collector's actions. Anyone not connected to the debt who was called by the collector is a useful person to have on your side because collectors are tightly restricted in these contacts. Collectors are permitted to call third parties only to obtain information on your whereabouts, or to leave a message. They aren't supposed to reveal that they are collecting a debt, or even to phone more than once unless they have reason to believe the person has new information that wasn't available in their first phone call. Even people in your household, that is, sharing your phone number, shouldn't be informed of the nature of the call, unless they share responsibility for the debt. One action brought by regulators in Maine brought out testimony from neighbors and coworkers of "debtors" to whom the collector had revealed information about the supposed debts. As in the Idaho case, that collector was barred from calling the state.[3]

So you need to know how to collect evidence—and how do you know what to collect? Blatant threats and lies are easiest to spot and carry the most weight in a courtroom. Any caller who threatens criminal prosecution and jail is the one violating the law. However, violations don't have to be as outrageous as those left on the Idaho resident's answering machine to provide support for an FDCPA case. Misrepresentation can be subtle. The use of legal terminology, for example, can falsely imply that the collector is associated with a law firm and that a lawsuit against the consumer is in the works. The law forbids collectors from using legal phrases that convey the impression of court action. Even calling your file or account a "case" is over the line.

Different collectors will likely call you about the same bill. This is part of their tactic to wear people down—persistence being a prime virtue of collectors. The idea is that a different tactic, even a different voice, will work to pry money from you where the first attempt failed. This variation can also work to your advantage. Among the bouquet of different collection tactics presented to you over the course of time, there are likely to be some noncompliant thorns.

Perhaps most important is what not to do. Victims of abusive collections are often outraged over things that aren't necessarily illegal. The condescending and disdainful tone of a collector and the implication that you are a person of low character for letting a bill go unpaid are things that leave people steaming. One woman in Indiana was incensed when a collector demanded that she pay debts racked up by her ex-husband on an old credit card. Under the terms of their divorce, the husband was responsible for the debts, she said. What's more, the ex-spouse was behind in paying his obligations to her. To be told—rudely—to pay off his old credit card charges sent her into apoplexy. Yet the collector might have a legal right to dun for joint debts taken on during marriage, regardless of the terms of a later property settlement. As unfair as it might be, a debt taken jointly by a couple during marriage can still be collected from either spouse, even if a subsequent divorce decree says that one or the other spouse is solely responsible for repayment. Focusing on such injustices where you do not have a firm legal claim, as bitter as they might be, will not help you land a consumer attorney or win your case.

25

Negotiating a Debt Settlement

Successful negotiation of a debt settlement can erase hundreds or perhaps even thousands of dollars from your obligations. Depending on the account and the creditor, collectors might be able to cancel half the balance or more. Therefore, once you have decided to settle a debt, it is worthwhile to prepare for the negotiation by combining all that we have learned about debt collectors, how they operate, and your rights in the collection process. To maximize your savings, it is necessary to keep in mind the pressures on the collector and what he or she already knows about you, as well as the provisions of the Fair Debt Collection Practices Act and the Fair Credit Reporting Act that govern the collection process.

To begin with, there are some costly mistakes to avoid:

- **Don't be pressured into acting quickly.** Collectors might emphasize that the settlement offer is about to expire, but this is rarely true. More likely, it is the individual collector who will lose the account if he or she fails to bring in a quick payment, so the pressure is on them. Your preferred time frame to lock in the settlement is near the end of the month, when the collector will be highly motivated to conclude a deal, and deeper discounts than usual might be available.

- **Don't jump at the first deal offered.** Most debts in collection, particularly credit card balances, are grossly inflated with penalty interest and fees. If the first collector who calls doesn't extend an offer that will wipe out most of these extras, you can probably make a better deal with someone else.

- **Don't give more information than the collector already has.** Your cell phone number, place of employment, and work phone number are highly desirable to the collector, who might ask for this information as a condition of a settlement. You have valid reasons for protecting this information. Remind the collector that your desire to protect your information is not an indication of bad faith, and has nothing to do with your intention to follow through with a fair settlement, if one is offered. The fact that the two of you are in communication shows that the collector needs no further contact information.

Before the negotiation even begins, you should review your records of the account. By this time, you should have gone through the FDCPA validation process to verify that this is a legitimate obligation. Also look on your credit report to check the amount reflected there. Then check your own records of the account. How much of the total due represents charges that you actually made and benefited from? How much is interest, penalty interest, and overlimit fees? Have any fees been tacked on by the collection agency, above and beyond charges from the original creditor? Knowing the answer to these questions will help you decide the target amount to accept in a settlement. It will also provide you with bargaining points in negotiations. Many debtors are surprised by the amount of fees and interest that have piggybacked on their charges. If a "collection fee" is tacked on, or post-charge-off interest, argue to get this removed entirely as a condition of discussing the account balance. The agency will be collecting a substantial portion of whatever settlement you pay, making additional fees difficult for them to defend. Moreover, depending on the terms of the original account and the laws in your state, such fees might also be open to legal challenge. One indication of a collection fee, if the collector fails to disclose it, is that the amount demanded is greater than the balance showing on your credit report. Demand that the collector explain any difference between the official account balance and the amount they claim.

Be aware that settlement rates will be much better for an upfront payment. Stretching payments out over a monthly cycle might be the only way to meet the obligation within your budget, but the collector probably will not agree to wipe out a portion of the debt to be paid over monthly installments.

That being said, however, an up-front settlement might not have to be paid all at once. It may be broken into "parts," or monthly payments of various sizes. For example, my agency would accept settlement payments in up to three parts, meaning the settlement amount could be split over three months. The danger here, however, was that missing any one of the payments would invalidate the settlement. Any partial payment the debtor made would be applied to the full balance, and negotiation to settle the remainder would have to begin again.

Once you have reviewed your account and your credit report, you are ready to bargain. At this stage of the game, it is important to be prepared for the lines of argument that a collector will make. Avoid being knocked off balance by aggressive demands so that you can stick to your agenda. The following are some tactics to expect and how to respond:

- You are legally and morally obligated to pay the balance, the collector will argue. The penalties and fees are the result of your own actions. You approved them when you signed the agreement that governs the account.

  Answer: Exorbitant penalties are not made fair by the fact that they were inserted into the small print of a credit agreement, whose prominent headline promised low monthly rates. Congress adopted the Credit CARD Act to restrict these practices going forward. What would be fair would be to make the law retroactive to include your balance within its protections. Offer to pay a fair amount that fits your budget.

- You are paying other bills; you have kept your (car/rent/mortgage) payment up to date; you must simply be ignoring this bill because you have resources to pay.

  Answer: It is necessary to prioritize bills. Obviously, the utilities, rent, or mortgage have greater priority than the unpaid bill. You might also need to keep your car payments up in order to be able to get to work. For these same reasons, you are unable to pay the full balance of the bill, but are willing to discuss a partial settlement that will allow you to continue to pay for necessities.

- Your credit record will deteriorate if you leave this bill unpaid.

  Answer: If the delinquency already appears on your credit report, the damage is done. (If more than 90 to 180 days delinquent, the bill has likely been reported by the creditor; and if charged-off, it almost certainly has been reported.) Paying it off sooner rather than later yields no special benefits to you. On the contrary, the delinquency should disappear from the report after seven years, under the U.S. Fair Credit Reporting Act.

- You can get the money to extinguish this debt from a loan company, advance on a paycheck, relatives, other lines of credit, or by skipping a mortgage payment.

  Answer: Taking on more debt, at higher interest, does not make economic sense. Nor does putting your home at risk to erase a bill. But, more important, the collector is only guessing that you have access to these other sources of funds. Argue that a workable settlement will need to match your real resources, not imaginary ones plucked by the collector out of thin air.

- Your choice is to pay this bill now or be taken to court and have it deducted from your pay or assets. The collector will likely try to keep the threat of court action in the background, at least implicitly, as an inducement to achieving a settlement.

  Answer: Your response to this will depend on your financial and legal position. Although the empty threat of court action is illegal, it is difficult to know what step the creditor might take next. Some debtors are indeed subject to court action eventually. Unfortunately, it is impossible to know in any given case what the odds are of facing a lawsuit to recover the debt. But the important thing to remember at this stage is that the collector, not being empowered to bring a lawsuit against you, does not likely know more than you do about what will happen next if you do not pay the bill. Ask the collector how he or she knows that court action will be taken. If the collector responds with an explicit threat of legal action, you probably have grounds for a complaint against the agency under the Fair Debt Collection Practices Act. Certainly, any threats of criminal action are false.

Once you have achieved the best settlement you can obtain, your next step is to lock it in. Get terms in writing. The terms should specify the account balance, the agreed settlement amount, and the phrase "settlement in full," meaning the debt is expunged. The terms should also specify the original account number as it appears on your statements from the creditor, not merely the number assigned to the account by the agency for their own internal tracking purposes.

In return for erasing a large portion of the balance, collectors will usually demand prompt action and same-day payment. Tell them that you are prepared to act promptly if they are; this puts the onus back on them and deprives them of the argument that you are employing a delaying tactic.

To conclude a deal involving several hundred dollars or more than $1,000, it is worthwhile to take on some extra minor effort and expense. Although you must have terms in writing to protect yourself, it is possible to conclude a settlement within 24 hours and still obtain complete documentation. Once you have received the collector's written terms of the settlement by fax, you may either overnight a check or wire money via an electronic transfer from your bank or a commercial service. If a check is being sent via overnight mail, you can provide the tracking number to the collector by phone, verifying that the payment is on the way. Thus, it is possible to conclude a same-day settlement as the collector demands, while still ensuring that you are protected with complete documentation of the terms.

The terms should also require the collector to report the settlement to the creditor and the credit reporting agencies so that it can be noted on your credit report. However, you will need to be prepared to do this yourself if the collector or creditor fails to follow through. That is one important reason for having full documentation of the settlement, to provide proof to the credit reporting agencies.

The fulfillment of the debt should be reflected on your credit report by the phrase "settlement in full." Creditors will understand that you paid less than the full account balance, and some might mark you down as a higher risk because of this. Some debtors opt to make payment in full for this reason. Obviously, the major disadvantage of doing so is the added expense. Furthermore, the period of delinquency will still be reflected on your report. Some sources of advice recommend that debtors negotiate a notation of "payment in full" from the collector rather than "settlement in full" as part of the settlement. However, reporting false information to a credit reporting agency is prohibited by the Fair Credit Reporting Act. The collector— and you—should be reluctant to cross that line. Other sources of advice recommend that you negotiate to have the delinquent account deleted from your report, instead of a settlement notation. However, this flatly contradicts the stated policy of credit reporting bureaus, which say they will delete only incorrect information.

Endnotes

Introduction

[1] Federal Trade Commission Annual Report: Fair Debt Collection Practices Act, 2005–2009.

[2] National Consumer Law Center comments to FTC on FDCPA enforcement, June 6, 2007.

[3] Federal Reserve Statistical Release, Consumer Credit, August 2009.

[4] "CAMCO to Pay $1 Million to Settle Unfair, Deceptive Debt Collection Practices," Federal Trade Commission news release, Dec. 5, 2004.

Chapter 2

[1] American Bankers Association, *Consumer Credit Delinquency Bulletin*, Second Quarter 2009.

[2] Eric Dash and Andrew Martin, "Banks Brace for Credit Card Write-Offs," *The New York Times*, May 10, 2009.

[3] Federal Reserve, "Changes in Family Finances, 2004–2007."

[4] Mark Whitehouse, "Household Debt Can Hasten Recovery, When It Goes Unpaid," *The Wall Street Journal*, Oct. 26, 2009.

[5] Federal Reserve Statistical Release, Consumer Credit, August 2009.

[6] Christian E. Weller, "Drowning in Debt: America's Middle Class Falls Deeper in Debt as Income Growth Slows and Costs Climb," Center for American Progress, Washington, D.C., May, 2006.

7 U.S. Government Accountability Office, "Credit Cards: Increased Complexity in Rates and Fees Heightens Need for More Effective Disclosures to Consumers," Sept. 21, 2006.

8 American Bankers Association, "Consumer Credit Delinquency Bulletin, Third Quarter 2009."

9 U.S. Bureau of Labor Statistics, "Occupational Employment and Wages," May 2008.

10 Federal Trade Commission Annual Report: The Fair Debt Collection Practices Act 2009.

11 U.S. Bureau of Labor Statistics *Occupational Outlook Handbook*, 2008–2009.

12 ACA International, "Collections Information from ACA," June 29, 2005.

13 NCO Group 10-K annual report to the SEC, March 31, 2009.

14 Rosa-Maria Gelpi, *The History of Consumer Credit*, St. Martin's Press Inc., 2000.

15 Robert M. Hunt, "Overview of the Collection Industry," Federal Reserve Bank of Philadelphia, Oct. 10 2007.

16 Minnesota Attorney General's Office, "Attorney General Takes Action Against Debt Collectors," news release June 16, 2004.

Chapter 5

1 Application for Resignation of J. Daniel Lenahan, New York State Appellate Division, Fourth Department, March 28, 2006.

2 Fred Williams, "Rogue Debt Collector Operated Under Watchdogs' Noses," *The Buffalo News*, July 24, 2006.

3 Deposition of Steven G. Munson, State of Maine v. Lenahan Law Offices LLC et al., Maine Superior Court Kennebec, Feb. 15, 2006.

4 Fred Williams, "Why Lenahan Discipline Case Took Years," *The Buffalo News*, Oct. 15, 2006.

5 Fred Williams, "Suit Says Two Area Bill Collectors Not Paying Their Bills," *The Buffalo News*, June 29, 2003.

6 "Credit Cards: Fair Debt Collection Practices Act Could Better Reflect the Evolving Debt Collection Marketplace and Use of Technology," U.S. Government Accountability Office, Sept. 2009 (GAO-09-748).

7 "CAMCO to Pay $1 Million to Settle Unfair, Deceptive Debt Collection Practices," U.S. Federal Trade Commission, Dec. 5, 2006.

8 *U.S. Federal Trade Commission v. Capital Acquisitions and Management Corp.* Complaint, Dec. 2, 2004, U.S. District Court Northern District of Illinois.

9 "Memorandum Supporting Plaintiff's Ex Parte Motion for Temporary Restraining Order, Other Equitable Relief, and Order to Show Cause Why a Preliminary Injunction Should Not Issue," Dec. 2, 2004, *FTC v. CAMCO*, U.S. District Court for Northern District of Illinois.

10 "Federal Trade Commission Annual Report: Fair Debt Collection Practices Act," U.S. Federal Trade Commission, 2003-2009.

11 "Nationwide Debt Collector Will Pay $2.25 Million to Settle FTC Charges," U.S. Federal Trade Commission, Nov. 21, 2008.

12 "Debt Collection Supervisors Settle FTC Charges," U.S. Federal Trade Commission, Jan. 7, 2010.

13 "Federal Trade Commission Annual Report: Fair Debt Collection Practices Act," U.S. Federal Trade Commission, 2003-2009.

14 Ray Huard, "Debt Collector Gets Jail for Extortion," *San Diego Union-Tribune*, Aug. 14, 2006.

15 Unpublished interview with Tricia Pummill, deputy District Attorney San Diego County, Aug. 15, 2006.

16 "Prosecution of Fraud Violations," San Diego County District Attorney's Office, Consumer Protection Unit.

17 Fred Williams, "Debt Police," *Kiplinger's Personal Finance*, Nov. 2006.

18 Affidavit of Adam Wisniewski, Platinum Recovery Services Inc. vs. Adam Wisniewski, City Court of the City of Niagara Falls, July 13, 2006.

19 Affidavit of Adam Wisniewski.

20 Unpublished interview with Adam Wisniewski.

21 Affidavit of Service, Brian T. Burgasser, Platinum Recovery vs. Wisniewski, Feb. 2, 2000.

22 Fred Williams, "Debt Police," *Kiplinger's Personal Finance*, Nov. 2006.

23 Fred Williams, "Debt Police," *Kiplinger's Personal Finance*, Nov. 2006.

24 Fred Williams, "When Collectors Call," *The Buffalo News*, Feb. 16, 2009.

Chapter 8

1 "Pelosi Statement on House Passage of Expedited CARD Reform for Consumers Act," Office of the Speaker of the House, Nov. 14, 2009.

2 "The Arbitration Trap: How Credit Card Companies Ensnare Consumers," *Public Citizen*, Sept. 27, 2007.

[3] "Credit card issuers defend use of arbitrators," The Associated Press, July 22, 2009.

[4] *Vandegenachte v. CRB*, U.S. District Court Western District of New York, Nov. 12, 2004.

Chapter 9

[1] *Harold Wood v. M & J Recovery et. al.*, U.S. District Court Eastern District of New York, Nov. 30, 2005.

[2] *Harold Wood v. M & J Recovery et. al.*, U.S. District Court Eastern District of New York, Nov. 30, 2005.

[3] "Global Debt Buying Report," Kaulkin Ginsberg, March 2006.

[4] Fred Williams "Wide-Open Market for Debts Feeds Abusive Tactics," *The Buffalo News*, July 25, 2006.

[5] Memorandum supporting plaintiff's ex parte motion for temporary restraining order, other equitable relief, and order to show cause why a preliminary injunction should not issue, *FTC v. CAMCO*, U.S. District Court Northern District of Illinois, Dec. 2, 2004.

[6] Fred Williams "Wide-Open Market for Debts Feeds Abusive Tactics," *The Buffalo News*, July 25, 2006.

[7] Fred Williams, "Merchants of Debt: Buffalo Debt Collectors Are Spreading Havoc," *The Buffalo News*, July 23, 2006; Fred Williams "Wide-Open Market for Debts Feeds Abusive Tactics," *The Buffalo News*, July 25, 2006.

Chapter 11

[1] "How Being in Debt Can Affect Your Military Career," Myvesta Org. Inc., May 17, 2004.

[2] "Scope and Impact of Personal Financial Management Difficulties of Service Members on the Department of the Navy," Military Family Institute, Marywood University, August 1997.

Chapter 14

[1] Federal Register notice: Regulation E final rule, Federal Reserve Board, Nov. 12, 2009.

[2] "Overdraft Explosion: Bank Fees for Overdrafts Increase 35% in Two Years," Center for Responsible Lending, Oct. 6, 2009.

[3] Andrew Martin, "Bank of America to End Debit Overdraft Fees," *The New York Times*, March 9, 2010.

Chapter 17

[1] *Nadine Frankenfield and Richard Frankenfield v. National Action Financial Services Inc., et al.*, U.S. District Court Eastern District of Pennsylvania, Jan. 20, 2004.

[2] *Frankenfield v. NAFS*, Memorandum, U.S. Magistrate Judge, Dec. 8, 2005.

[3] Unpublished interview with Peter Barry, attorney for Frankenfield.

Chapter 19

[1] Remarks by the President at signing of the Credit Card Accountability, Responsibility, and Disclosure Act, White House press release, May 22, 2009.

[2] "Collecting Consumer Debts: The Challenges of Change," Federal Trade Commission, February 2009.

[3] "FTC Workshop Reveals Modernization of Debt Collection Laws Needed," ACA International, Oct. 12, 2007.

[4] "Consumer Price Index All Urban Consumers, 1947-," U.S. Department of Labor Bureau of Labor Statistics, compiled at Federal Reserve Bank of St. Louis, Federal Reserve Economic Data (FRED) Database.

[5] "Credit Cards: Fair Debt Collection Practices Act Could Better Reflect the Evolving Debt Collection Marketplace and Use of Technology," U.S. Government Accountability Office, September 2009.

[6] "Levin: GAO Report on Credit Card Debt Collection Problems Highlights Need for Consumer Financial Protection Agency," Sen. Carl Levin's Office, Oct. 21, 2009.

Chapter 20

[1] Robert M. Hunt, "Overview of the Collection Industry," Federal Reserve Bank of Philadelphia, Oct. 10, 2007.

Chapter 21

[1] "Collecting Consumer Debts: The Challenges of Change," FTC, February 2009.

[2] "Collecting Consumer Debts: The Challenges of Change," FTC, February 2009.

Chapter 22

[1] Fred Williams, "Firm's Debt-Collection Tactics Decried," *The Buffalo News*, Oct. 3, 2004.

[2] "Collecting Consumer Debts: The Challenges of Change," FTC, February 2009.

Chapter 23

[1] "Mistakes Do Happen: A Look at Errors in Consumer Credit Reports," U.S. Public Interest Research Group, June, 2004.

Chapter 24

[1] Interview with William N. Lund, director, Maine Office of Consumer Credit Regulation, Feb. 21, 2006.

[2] Cease and Desist Order, Idaho Department of Finance, *Consumer Finance Bureau v. Giove Law Office PC*, Oct. 15, 2004.

[3] Fred Williams, "Firm's Debt Collection Tactics Decried," *The Buffalo News*, Oct. 3, 2004.

INDEX